50 GREATS
GREATS
CASTLEFORD
RUGBY LEAGUE CLUB

Five Castleford Great Britain tourists from 1970. From left to right: Dennis Hartley, Keith Hepworth, Alan Hardisty, Derek Edwards and Malcolm Reilly.

50 GREATS

CASTLEFORD
RUGBY LEAGUE CLUB

COMPILED BY
DAVID SMART
&
ANDY HOWARD

TEMPUS

First published 2002, reprinted 2003
Copyright © David Smart & Andy Howard, 2002

Tempus Publishing Limited
The Mill, Brimscombe Port,
Stroud, Gloucestershire, GL5 2QG

ISBN 0 7524 2430 0

TYPESETTING AND ORIGINATION BY
Tempus Publishing Limited
PRINTED IN GREAT BRITAIN BY
Midway Colour Print, Wiltshire

Present and forthcoming rugby titles from Tempus Publishing:

0 7524 2702 4	Barrow RLFC	Keith Nutter	£10.99
0 7524 2717 2	Bristol RFC: 1945-2002	Mark Hoskins & Dave Fox	£10.99
0 7524 2429 7	Hull RLFC: 100 Greats	Raymond Fletcher	£12.00
0 7524 2709 1	Neath RFC: 1871-1945	Mike Price	£10.99
0 7524 2703 2	Pontypool RFC	Ray Ruddick	£10.99
0 7524 2706 7	St Helens RLFC: Classic Matches	Alex Service	£12.00
0 7524 2721 0	Swansea RFC: 1873-1945	Bleddyn Hopkins	£10.99
0 7524 2708 3	Swinton RLFC	Stephen Wild	£10.99
0 7524 2414 9	Warrington RLFC: 100 Greats	Gary Slater	£12.00

Acknowledgements

Tracking down pictures for this book has been a labour of love for Andy, but would not have been possible without the huge help, support and patience of the following people.
We would like say many thanks to:

Brian Kent, Mrs Fox, Clive Hinton, Mrs Newton, David Newton, Mrs Philips, Robert Gate, Harry Edgar, Len Garbutt, John Kendrew, Alan Hardisty, Brian Lockwood, Bill Bryant, Peter Small, Denzil Webster, Sig Kasatkin, Giles Boothroyd, the staff of the Yorkshire Post Picture Library, *Pontefract & Castleford Express*, Varley Picture Agency, Mike Brett, Neil Underwood and Grandad Fred, Emma and Matt Gill, Steve Smith, David, Pauline and Vicki Lloyd, Graeme Harvey, Sarah Roberts, Richard Wright, Steve Parker, Gordon Howard, Paul Haithwaite, Michael Turner, Gerald Webster, League Publications Ltd and Sports Photo Agency.

If we have missed any names from this list or have infringed any copyright, it as been done so unknowingly.

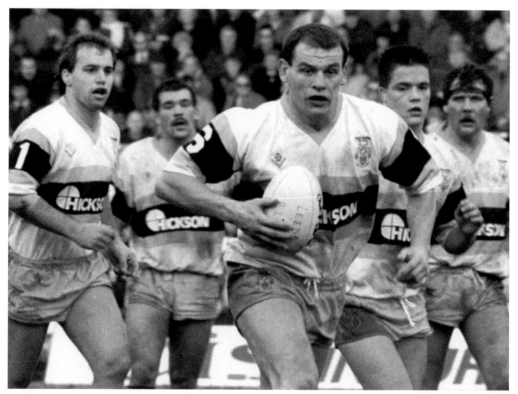

Leading from the front. John Joyner – club captain, Great Britain International and an inspiration to a generation of Castleford players – in action at Headingley, Boxing Day 1990. Also pictured, from left to right: Steve Larder, Keith England, Graham Southernwood, Kevin Beardmore.

Jim 'Ginger' Crossley moves in to assist Tommy Askin in the ground breaking 1935 match in France versus Lyon.

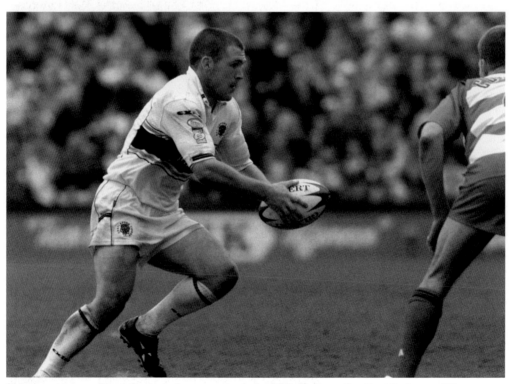

Sixty-seven years on Danny Orr looks for an opening in the 2002 Challenge Cup Semi-Final versus Wigan.

Introduction

Deciding who should be featured in this book appeared to be an easy task, with each of us quickly scribbling down around twenty names. Those were our choices but we would guess that the same names would feature on the lists of most people who have followed Castleford over the years. The next ten came relatively easily, but by now you would also to have been a Castleford supporter of a certain age to be likely to agree with them. And from there, it became progressively harder to arrive at our fifty, because there have been hundreds of 'Greats' who have donned the Castleford jersey.

We should add that by no means do we claim these fifty players to have been the greatest ever to have played for the club. For some, their greatness has been enhanced by being part of a great side. Others have been less fortunate, never winning honours, but shining through the club's thin times. Some may not have been outstandingly gifted players, but they have shown loyalty and commitment to the club over many years. And then there are a few who were only with us briefly, but provided great entertainment.

Thankfully, Castleford historian Len Garbett gave us the benefit of his vast knowledge in selecting which players to include from the club's early history, and I am indebted for some of his words. However, the rest of the players have been decided upon by Andy and me, and we weren't too far apart when, independently, listing our initial choices.

Readers will undoubtedly have their own thoughts, but it was inevitably a subjective project settling on the fifty. Whoever might have been our fifty-first and fifty-second choices, and beyond, could have been equally great – but a line had to be drawn somewhere.

We hope that some debate has been stimulated.

David Smart & Andy Howard

NB The points values of tries and drop goals in the game of Rugby League have changed over the years and therefore the point tallies may not reconcile with today's value. The figures in brackets by the number of appearances represent the number of substitute appearances made.

Kevin (foreground) and Bob Beardmore directing play at Wheldon Road.

50 Castleford Greats

Les Adams	Alan Lowndes
Arthur Atkinson	Albert Lunn
Robert and Kevin Beardmore	Tony Marchant
Richie Blackmore	*Roger Millward*
Bill Bryant	*Tawera Nikau*
Bruce Burton	*Steve Norton*
Lee Crooks	*Danny Orr*
Jim Crossley	David Plange
Jim Croston	Ken Pye
Derek Edwards	Stuart Raper
St John Ellis	Mick Redfearn
Keith England	*Malcolm Reilly*
Mike Ford	*Dean Sampson*
Ronnie Gibbs	John Sheridan
Alan Hardisty	Peter Small
Dennis Hartley	Bob Spurr
Keith Hepworth	*Graham Steadman*
Barry Johnson	Gary Stephens
John Joyner	Nathan Sykes
Bill Kirkbride	Thomas Taylor
George Langfield	Darryl Van De Velde
George Lewis	Adrian Vowles
Bob Lindner	Johnny Ward
Geoff Lloyd	*Kevin Ward*
Brian Lockwood	Geoff Wraith

The twenty who appear here in italics occupy three pages instead of the usual two.

Les Adams
Scrum-half, 1933-1942

Appearances: 196

Tries: 39

Goals: 0

Drop Goals: 0

Points: 117

Previous club: Huddersfield

When Castleford signed Les Adams from Huddersfield in the 1933/34 season, they acquired a Challenge Cup veteran and a winner. Rejoicing in the nickname of 'Juicy', Adams was a lively scrum half who had first tasted cup glory with Leeds when they won the competition in 1932, defeating Swinton 11-8. Unfortunately, he missed out on a Wembley appearance, as three years after the Rugby League had taken the brave decision to move their showcase match to London, the 1932 final date caused a problem for the soccer authorities. Although the FA Cup final was actually scheduled to take place a week after the date of rugby's final, the Football Association had an agreement with Wembley that no match could be played at the ground in the seven days preceding it. The rugby final was earlier than usual as there was a tour to Australia scheduled, and, in those days, it wasn't a twenty-hour flight to Sydney – more like a forty-day boat trip! So, with no compromise possible, the match was played at Wigan's Central Park. Twelve months later though, Adams was to tread the hallowed turf. A transfer to Huddersfield in the close season proved the key as his new club battled through to the semi-final. Their opponents were Adams former club, Leeds, but Huddersfield triumphed and won the

right to face Warrington in the final – this time at Wembley. Interestingly, the crowd at almost 42,000 was 13,000 up on the previous year's attendance at Wigan. And, for good measure, Huddersfield won, defeating Warrington, to give Adams his second winner's medal.

Just over a year after making his Castleford debut, against Wigan in January 1934, Adams, one of Castleford's finest scrum-halves, was on his way to a third winner's medal. Cas had fought their way to Wembley for their first ever final in 1935, and Adams was to face his former side in Huddersfield. A key player in the final, Adams scored a vital try as underdogs Cas hung on to win 11-8. Three teams, three cup finals and three winner's medals for 'Juicy' Adams.

In 1939, Adams almost led Castleford to more glory in the club's first ever Championship final. With skipper Arthur Atkinson injured, Adams took over the captaincy for the clash with Salford at Maine Road, but there was no Challenge Cup-style fairytale on this occasion, as the Red Devils snatched a narrow 8-6 victory in front of a

Les Adams in action at Wembley in 1935.

Les Adams is introduced to the guests at the 1935 cup final.

massive attendance of almost 70,000 supporters.

Adams was already an international when he joined the club, having represented Great Britain against Australia whilst at Leeds, and he went on to win two England and six Yorkshire caps in his time with Castleford. Those matches for England came three years apart, both against Wales and both ending in defeat for the Cas star.

Having moved around somewhat in his early career, Les Adams stuck with Cas for the rest of his playing days. But tragically he was one of the many casualties of the Second World War. He served in the Royal Air Force and was reported missing over Burma.

Arthur Atkinson

Centre three-quarter, 1926-1942

Appearances: 431

Tries: 157

Goals: 230

Drop Goals: 1

Points: 933

Previous club: Local junior rugby

Many of Castleford's older generation of supporters to this day regard Arthur Atkinson as the club's finest ever player. In truth, there are few in a position to argue, but statistics suggest that it is more than memories of halcyon days gone by that earn him this status.

Atkinson made his Castleford debut on 11 September 1926, in the club's fourth match following their admittance to the Northern Rugby Football League that year. Still a teenager, the match was away to Rochdale, and it was a losing start to young Atkinson's career as the Hornets won 33-5. However, it was also the start of a glittering career which spanned sixteen years and just one club, Castleford. Atkinson's name is still held in high regard today – even by some whose fathers were too young to have actually seen him play!

His first of many tries for Castleford came a month after his debut, against Halifax, and, as he was also a good goalkicker, he remains one of the club's most prolific scorers seventy-six years later. He was denied one score though, in a fashion that led to the Rugby League having to make a rule change. Cas were playing Swinton at home in the Challenge Cup quarter-final and Arthur was racing away for a touchdown. But one of the Lions players, who was off the field having treatment for an injury, ran back on to the field and tackled him. As a result of this incident, the law was changed, with permission now having to be sought from an official before a player can return after treatment. It was too late for Castleford, however, who lost the tie 0-3.

Although Arthur played a number of times at full-back and on the wing, with odd appearances at stand-off and in the pack, his position was centre. It was there that he shone like a beacon, as his Castleford side – he took over the captaincy in season 1928/29 – sought to establish themselves in those early days in the club's history. In fact, Atkinson was himself making history and, in November 1929, he became the first ever Castleford player to be selected for Great Britain, playing against Australia at Leeds in a match that the 'home' side won 9-3. He was a GB tryscorer that day and went on to score a further 5 tries in another 10 Test matches, as well as being Castleford's first tourist to Australasia in 1932 – a trip he made again in 1936. Arthur also made 6 appearances for England and 14 for the Yorkshire County side. One of those

Atkinson in his 1935 Wembley kit.

Captain Arthur Atkinson leads his victorious cup-winning side of 1935.

England appearances was against Australia but was played in Paris in 1933 – the first Rugby League match to be played in France. Atkinson's debut for Yorkshire, perhaps inevitably as the first Castleford player to represent the White Rose outfit, came in Cardiff when Glamorgan & Monmouth were the opposition – and we talk of expansion these days.

However, despite all of those representative honours, Atkinson's finest hour came in 1935 when he led his side to their first Wembley appearance and to victory. Castleford had gone close to making a Wembley appearance in 1929, just three years after their admittance to the League, only to be denied by Dewsbury in the semifinal. But six years later, they weren't to be denied with victory over Barrow in the semifinal taking Arthur Atkinson and his men to Wembley. It wasn't a classic match, but in overcoming the favourites, Huddersfield, Castleford took the cup in what was a proud day for the club and the town. So often a match-winner, skipper Atkinson had a moderate game by his own very high standards, but was the first man to lift a trophy for Cas and, indeed, the last for many years.

Throughout his career, Atkinson was a standard-bearer for the club, and his final game for Cas came in March 1942 – like his first, it ended in defeat. The opposition was Keighley, and they spoilt his finale by recording a 13-0 victory.

Sadly Arthur Atkinson, the first Castleford legend, died in 1963 when he was just fifty-seven, on the day of his wedding anniversary. The club erected the Arthur Atkinson Memorial Gates as a tribute and they remain at the ground to this day.

Kevin & Robert Beardmore

Kevin: Hooker, 1979-1992

Kevin Beardmore

Appearances: 241(6)

Tries: 80

Goals: 0

Drop Goals: 0

Points: 297

Previous club: Local junior rugby

Amongst the best and most popular players ever to represent Castleford, Robert and Kevin Beardmore must be Rugby League's most famous twins. Both of these great talents signed for the club from local amateur side Fryston, Kevin, a hooker, joined in November 1977 and Bob, a scrum-half, five months later. In both cases, they were fulfilling long-held ambitions. Although Kevin had been the first to sign, Bob progressed more quickly and, in 1979, he twice represented the Great Britain Colts side – the forerunner of today's academy set-up. Kevin, though, was finding Bob Spurr, himself a top-class player for Cas, a tough man to displace from the first-team hooking spot. As a result, it was Bob who first broke through to make his senior Castleford debut in November 1979. Kevin did follow him into the first team shortly afterwards, but, despite impressing, he was still unable to oust Spurr on a regular basis. Indeed, Bob's path to regular first-team football was also being blocked by another quality player in Gary Stephens, but he continued to press and his tremendous potential was eventually recognised, as the club felt able to sell Gary Stephens to Wigan, early in the 1980/81 campaign. Bob didn't

waste the opportunity and as a regular first-team player (and a tremendous goalkicker, scoring plenty of points), he won his first senior medal when Cas defeated Bradford in the 1981 Yorkshire Cup final. However, for twin Kevin, injury problems and the continued good form of Bob Spurr continued to deny him a place.

Season 1982/83, whilst being a somewhat disappointing one for the Castleford club, proved a watershed for the Beardmores, with Bob notching 276 points during the campaign and Kevin, at long last, clinching a regular first-team place. Kevin quickly emulated his brother in becoming a key member of the Castleford line-up, and he too showed that he could score points, proving to have a real eye for the try-line. In only his second full season, he was also proving that he could match the best and it was no surprise when, at the season's end, he gained selection for the 1984 Great Britain squad that was to tour Australia. The surprise, and disappointment, was that Bob wasn't making it a family affair. And for Kevin, despite the joy of selection, as the Lions' skipper Brian Noble was also a specialist hooker, there were few Test opportunities. But he did win his first cap, as a substitute against New Zealand, in the first of 15 international appearances for GB and England. Bob was never to win senior representative honours, although he was in the 1985 GB training squad, but, throughout his career, he was regarded as one of the best uncapped players

Robert Beardmore

Appearances: 279(14)

Tries: 99

Goals: 518

Drop Goals: 9

Points: 1,397

Previous club: Local junior rugby

in the game. Kevin though was once against to taste life Down Under in 1985 when he had a short guest spell with the Canberra Raiders club, in order to 'test himself' at the highest level.

The pinnacle of the twins' career was still to come, however. Throughout the 1985/86 campaign, Castleford were struggling, there was talk of financial worries, and Kevin was sidelined by injury for a long spell. But despite those problems, the club was about to embark upon their best Challenge Cup run for sixteen years – one that was to take them all the way to Wembley success. Kevin's injury meant that he missed out on all of the cup rounds, and even after the semi-final victory over Oldham, it was a race against time for him to recover for the final against Hull KR. Although it spelt disappointment for his very capable replacement, Stuart Horton, Kevin was ready in time to make the final, and it was a proud moment when the twins took to the field for their hometown club at Wembley. It was enough that Cas took the cup, but, fittingly, the Man of the Match award (the Lance Todd Trophy) went to Bob and was perhaps some consolation for those missing representative honours.

The momentum of Wembley was carried through to the following term and Hull were defeated in a pulsating Yorkshire Cup final, this with time Kevin taking the Man of the Match honours. However, although Kevin was adding to his representative honours, club success began to wane, yet Bob registered a

Division One points in a match record with 38 (4 tries and 11 goals) against Barrow. He had a couple more years at Castleford, which were relatively uneventful, but the wind of change was blowing through the club.

The twins enjoyed a well-deserved record-breaking benefit year in 1988, illustrating their popularity in Castleford. But Bob wasn't featuring too regularly in the first team and, in the 1989 off-season, he left, for what was to be a brief spell with Leigh, in a £35,000 transfer deal. Bob had kicked over 500 goals for Cas and amassed almost 1,400 points, with his massive total of 334 points in the 1983/84 season still a club record. Kevin stayed a while longer before he too, rather quietly, called it a day, after playing just one match in an injury-hit 1991/92 campaign. At that point, he and his brother had contributed a combined total of over twenty-five years top-class and loyal service to Castleford.

Including Bob and Kevin together in this book means that we have cheated a little because it should, in truth, be entitled *51 Greats*. But for the Beardmore twins, it couldn't have been done any other way.

Richie Blackmore

Centre three-quarter, 1991-1995

Appearances: 108(3)

Tries: 64

Goals: 0

Drop Goals: 0

Points: 256

Previous club: Otahuhu (New Zealand)

When Richie Blackmore signed for Castleford in 1991, he was hailed as one of New Zealand's most exciting young stars. The centre who, at 6ft 2in and 15st, was built like a forward, had starred for the Kiwis in their victory over Australia three weeks before his move, and he was rated as being very hot property. The twenty-one-year-old had, in fact, started his rugby life in the pack, but that was in Union as a flanker. He switched to League and had only been playing the thirteen-a-side code for two years, with the Otahuhu club in his native Auckland, when he made that Test bow.

Blackmore's Castleford debut came against St Helens at Knowsley Road in September 1991, but his eagerly awaited first appearance for the club lasted barely two minutes before he dislocated his shoulder! However, he was soon back in action, although medical opinion suggested that he was taking a gamble, and, after returning in a substitute appearance the week before, he played in the Tigers 1991 Yorkshire Cup-winning team. A cup final after just 45 minutes for Cas and a winner's medal after 125 wasn't a bad start for the young Kiwi. And, as the Challenge Cup com-petition got underway, things got even better. A tryscorer in the first and third rounds, Richie played a big part in Castleford's march to Wembley to face Wigan in 1992. The holders proved too strong on the day, as they were for every team at that time, but Richie was a Tigers tryscorer on the hallowed turf to round off a first campaign that had brought him so much. To cap things off, much to the delight of the Castleford fans, he agreed a new three-year contract. But even that wasn't the end for Richie for over the summer, back home in New Zealand, he featured in the Kiwis side that faced the GB tourists, bringing him face-to-face with one of the British stars, his team-mate Graham Steadman.

Back in the UK for Castleford's domestic campaign, Blackmore's star continued to shine brightly. 'One of Castleford's most inspired overseas signings' said the *Yorkshire Post*, after Richie had notched a hat-trick of tries in a 54-0 Regal Trophy victory for the Tigers against Carlisle. The big centre was certainly a handful for any defence, but injury wiped out a large chunk of his second year at the club: a key factor in what wasn't a bad season, but one that fell short of the previous year's glory.

The following season, 1993/94, saw John Joyner take up the coaching reins at Cas, and he augmented the Kiwi contingent of Blackmore and Nikau with the signing of another New Zealand Test player, Tony

Kemp. The trio certainly worked well together on the field on behalf of their adopted home town. Ironically, the New Zealand touring party were in England, but only Nikau of the Cas trio was selected by his country for the first Test at Wembley. That date against Great Britain caused him to miss the Tigers clash with the Kiwis, but it was not so for Richie or Tony Kemp, who both shone against their fellow countrymen as Castleford defeated the tourists 16-4. With a big point to make, Richie did so in style, laying on three of Castleford's four tries. However, whilst Kemp was called up by the Kiwis for the second Test, Richie, to some amazement, again missed out. It was all the more surprising as the Tigers were going so well, winning the Stones Bitter Team of the Month at the time of the tour, with Richie playing a big part.

In the lead-up to the third Test, he scored 6 tries in 4 games for Cas and at last he grabbed the Kiwi selectors' attention – his selection for the third Test side was richly deserved. Interestingly enough, that match saw the axing of New Zealand's brilliant scrum-half Gary Freeman, a player who ten years earlier had played superbly in an all-too-brief stint at Castleford. With the tourists back home, it was back to business for the England-based Kiwis, and for Castleford, it was the year of their last major success with their Regal Trophy final victory over Wigan. Richie was an integral part of that team and he scored his fair share of tries, finishing on 20 for the season. However, he was out-stripped by St John Ellis in that department, who was on his way to a new club record of 40 tries for the season. Yet whilst Ellis did tremendously well to reach that total, it is no coincidence that his centre partner was Richie Blackmore, who performed his role almost to perfection, and played a big part in creating the record.

The following year, though, saw a number of changes in the Tigers' make-up and, whilst Blackmore was going well (including scoring a try for Cas against the Australian tourists), rumours started to emerge about another change – his future. As early as January, there was speculation that clubs in Australia and New Zealand had put him on their wanted list. Richie was out of contract at the end of the year and, although Cas desperately wanted him to stay, it was to no avail. By February, it was confirmed that he was on his way out at the end of the campaign – to join the Auckland Warriors. The Tigers' season ended amidst the Super League debate, but Richie left as the leading tryscorer (scoring 24 for the season), as well as having made the most appearances (37). He had served the club well.

Richie was later to return for a second spell in the UK, this time with Leeds. Castleford had, reportedly, tried to bring him back to the club, but it didn't happen. He would certainly have been given a warm welcome by the Tigers' fans.

Richie Blackmore on the attack in the 1992 Challenge Cup final.

17

Appearances: 251(2)

Tries: 75

Goals: 0

Drop Goals: 0

Points: 225

Previous club: Local junior rugby

Bill Bryant was probably born a few years too soon. That fact, coupled with cruel luck in terms of injuries, cost 'Big' Bill the honours that he so richly deserved. Bill was from neighbouring Normanton and joined Castleford in 1957. His debut came the following year at home to Keighley, the club he was eventually to join twelve years later, and he played alongside older brother Eddie, who had joined Cas the year before Bill. Being between the two towns, Normanton youngsters at the time usually gravitated towards Wakefield or Castleford and, before signing for Cas, Bill had actually been playing for Trinity's juniors. However, his older brother's presence at Wheldon Road probably influenced his decision. Whilst never matching Bill's achievements, Eddie served Castleford well and went on to make 62 appearances, as well as perhaps being instrumental in Bill joining the club!

Bill started to emerge as a strong-running back-row forward, but it was fully four years before he cemented a regular place in the Castleford pack. But by the time he did, he was a mighty forward, who certainly knew his way to the try-line. Unfortunately, at the time, although the likes of Alan Hardisty and Keith Hepworth were beginning to make their mark in the backline, the Cas pack wasn't as strong as it might have been. In fact, at times it seemed that Bill was taking on the opposing forwards single-handed, especially in some of the big games. He took a lot of stick, but always came back for more, and it was just reward when, in 1964, Bill was chosen to play for Great Britain and made his Test debut against France. A year later, he made the first of his 6 appearances for Yorkshire and, in 1966, came what was to prove the pinnacle of his career – selection for Britain's tour to Australia and New Zealand. He twice played in Tests against the Aussies, revelling in such top-class company, but that taste of glory was to prove his last. The Castleford club was moving upwards and, with the signing of Dennis Hartley and the emergence of youngsters like Reilly and Lockwood, the pack was building into a formidable unit. The stage should have been set for well-deserved club honours, which for Bill had only come via three BBC2 Floodlit Cup wins. Tragically though, Bill's career was blighted by injury and, by January 1969, as Castleford were on the eve of the cup trail that was to take them to Wembley, he broke his leg for the third time

Bill Bryant dives over for a spectacular try.

Bill Bryant in caricature in the local paper.

in two years. Bill was to miss out on the glory that he aspired to and deserved. In 1970, Bill left the club and had a spell with Keighley. He went on to became a publican in Castleford before opening a bar in Tenerife, which, with a collection of memorabilia decking the walls, became a popular spot for Cas fans holidaying on the Spanish island. Sadly for Bill, those memorabilia didn't include the number of medals that he richly deserved.

Bill Bryant crosses for a try at Headingley.

Bruce Burton

Stand-off half, 1976-1980

Appearances: 134(1)

Tries: 89

Goals: 41

Drop Goals: 4

Points: 353

Previous club: Halifax

A then club record signing for Castleford, at a time when the club didn't spend too much, Bruce Burton turned out to be worth every penny, as he starred in many a match before injury prematurely ended an impressive career.

Burton's first Rugby League club was Halifax, whom he joined from Sandal RU, and he quickly became a Thrum Hall favourite. A brilliant individual player, who was the Man of the Match when Halifax won the John Player trophy in 1972, Burton was a top kicker, who, again in 1972, set the Halifax record of 14 in a single game. However, in 1976, Cas stepped in to pay £8,000 for the much sought-after stand-off star and Burton was on his way to Wheldon Road. Ironically, Bradford had made a bigger bid for Burton, offering £9,000, but that was reported to be on the basis of a down payment with the remainder on credit. Cas offered cash up front and won the day!

Burton scored on his Castleford debut against Hull KR, the first of many tries for the club, of which a significant amount were brilliant efforts. He had good hands and real pace, which he used to very good effect, never more so than in 1977 when Castleford won the Yorkshire Cup for the first time in their history. Burton scored the Tigers' two tries, adding a drop goal for good measure,

as local rivals Featherstone Rovers were defeated 17-7 in a performance that won him the White Rose Trophy as Man of the Match. His second try in particular was outstanding.

However, even before that Burton had been a massive influence in Castleford's double trophy year in the 1976/77 campaign. In the Players competition, he crossed twice for Cas in each of the first three rounds, which included wins at Knowsley Road and Headingley, and then again in the final against Blackpool Borough, ending the underdogs' hopes and brave resistance with a 60-yard special. In the successful Floodlit Trophy campaign, Burton scored in every round, including the win over Leigh in the final, ending the season with 29 tries in all competitions.

The following year, Bruce won the Castleford Player of the Year award, and another year on, he was again the club's leading scorer. However, things weren't going as well as they might have done. In the 1979 campaign, having added a Yorkshire appearance to his GB Under-24 honours, when he captained his country,

Classy half-back Bruce Burton in action in 1977.

Burton suffered a hamstring injury that kept him out of action for some weeks. He then he stunned the club by announcing that he had quit the game, reportedly citing the club's 'lack of interest in rebuilding the team' as a factor. A big-money bid from Hull was rejected, as Cas tried to persuade Burton to return to the club and, shortly afterwards, he did just that. But the old sparkle was never rekindled and further injuries, along with work commitments, brought Burton's career to an end in 1980. Sadly, that was without winning anything like the representative honours that he might have done and the Castleford fans were robbed of a jewel of a player who was only able to shine relatively briefly for the club.

Burton makes a typical break.

Lee Crooks
Prop forward, 1990-1997

Appearances: 215(7)

Tries: 18

Goals: 596

Drop Goals: 1

Points: 1,265

Previous club: Leeds

A legend on Humberside whilst still a teenager, Lee Crooks proved to be a tremendous signing for Castleford in 1990 by the then coach Darryl Van De Velde, especially as he was captured from arch-rivals Leeds. It's true that 'Crooksy' didn't have the happiest of times at Headingley, but he was on a reported ten-year contract and the Leeds chairman at the time of his move to Cas was quoted as saying: 'We did everything possible to try and keep Lee Crooks.'

Lee was a Hull boy who graduated through the schools and then academy ranks at the Boulevard. He won honours throughout his career, captaining Great Britain Schoolboys and then the Great Britain Academy Colts side on their first ever tour of Australia. At just eighteen years of age, he trod the hallowed Wembley turf for Hull in their 1982 drawn Challenge Cup final with Widnes. He came on as a second-half substitute in that match, but in the replay at Elland Road, young Crooks was on from the start. He played a major role, the first of many, with a try and three goals, as Hull took the cup for only the second time in their long history, after a gap of sixty-eight years. Incidentally, the curtain-raiser to that match saw the Hull Schools side take on Wigan in the England Schools Under-13 Championship final and at stand-off for the Humberside youngsters was the Tigers' current full-back Richard Gay.

However, that wasn't to be the end of Lee Crooks' achievements that year because by October, at just nineteen, he was making his Great Britain debut against the all-conquering Australian tourists in his hometown. The test was played at Boothferry Park, the home of the local soccer team, Hull City. Unfortunately, he couldn't help GB stop an outstanding team of Aussies.

However, Lee continued to have great success with Hull, winning further club and personal honours and amassing almost 1,000 points for the club and as such his transfer to Leeds in June 1987 was a major shock. It was suggested that Hull had to sell because of financial problems and equally it was said that Lee didn't want to leave the Humberside club, but with Leeds paying a cheque for £150,000, he made the move to Headingley. There were lots of rumours and speculation during Lee's time with Leeds, and it's true that his form did dip from his own high standards, but, whatever the precise reasons were, he didn't seem happy at the club. Unfortunately, one of his best performances for the Loiners came in the 1988 Yorkshire Cup final when Leeds beat Cas! However, as the 1989/90 season unfolded, there were suggestions that Lee, who lived in the town, might be on his way to Castleford, who under Darryl Van De Velde were becoming a club that was prepared to spend big money to bring top talent to Wheldon Road. So it was to prove, as, in January 1980, Lee opted to quit Headingley and make the move to Cas, with Leeds recouping the £150,000 that they had paid Hull. Amazingly, Featherstone Rovers had stepped in with a late bid of £170,000 for his services, which Leeds accepted, but Lee didn't want to move to Post Office Road. His heart was set on joining Castleford – and who could blame him?

He didn't make an auspicious start at his new club, incurring an eight-match ban after an incident in a match against Hull at the Boulevard, which curtailed his first term with the Tigers. From then on though, it was success all the way, as Lee settled at Cas in a way that he had been unable to at Leeds. A great leader, he was soon appointed the club's captain and led his side to success in the 1990 Yorkshire Cup final. In 1992, he was back at Wembley, but his Castleford side couldn't upset the holders and hot favourites Wigan, despite a battling display. His own form was top-drawer though, and it was no surprise when he added to his GB caps, taking his eventual tally to 19. Lee also made his third tour

Action from the 1992 Challenge Cup final, as Lee Crooks takes on Wigan's Billy McGinty.

Lee Crooks typically looking for a player in support.

Down Under in 1992 and played his only match for England.

Perhaps the highlight of Lee's seven years with Cas came when his side destroyed Wigan in the 1994 Regal Trophy final. 'Crooksy' led his side magnificently, producing an inspirational display as the red-hot pre-match favourites were torn apart. That match captured both his own playing ability and his leadership qualitites.

When Lee called it a day in 1997, the effects of various knee injuries finally catching up with him, he had played in 222 matches for the Tigers and notched 597 goals. In his Rugby League career, he had recorded no less than 1,060 goals and reached 2,387 points.

Not surprisingly, Lee went into coaching but, despite his best efforts, was unable to gain too much success under testing circumstances at both Keighley and York. These days he is still very much in the game, working on junior development in the Wakefield District, and, if the youngsters he is dealing with aspire to achieve a fraction of what Lee did, they will do very well.

Jim Crossley

Back-row forward, 1933-1949

Appearances: 261

Tries: 23

Goals: 6

Drop Goals: 2

Points: 85

Previous club: Local junior rugby

Jim 'Ginger' Crossley was one of Castleford's earliest 'greats', making his first-team debut in 1934 at just eighteen years of age. The match was against Huddersfield, but it wasn't a great start for the young forward, ending as it did in a heavy home defeat. Crossley served the club for sixteen years, spending almost all of his career in the back row, and he has the distinction of being the only Castleford player to appear in both their first ever Challenge Cup final (in 1935) and their first ever Yorkshire Cup final (in 1948). Being a part of that 1935 team gave Jim the distinction of being amongst the first thirteen Castleford players to appear at Wembley, and a win over Huddersfield meant that they didn't go away empty handed.

That impressive sixteen-year spell of service at Castleford is an achievement bettered only by John Joyner but Jim's appearances for the club weren't as many as they might have been due to the intervention of the Second World War. Jim, as did most young men, served his country, which caused him to miss some games, and, in any event, the war meant that Castleford didn't

field a team in either the 1942/43 or 1943/44 seasons.

Jim wasn't the biggest of forwards, but he commanded a great deal of respect from his opponents, and when Castleford faced the touring Australians in 1948, he was one of four players (two from each side) sent off in a rugged encounter.

When Jim finally called it a day, after playing against Dewsbury in April 1949, he closed another chapter in Castleford's history, as the last member of that 1935 cup-winning team to retire from playing for the club. Unfortunately, his senior career ended as it had begun, in defeat.

When his playing days were over, Jim continued at the club, taking over the role of second-team coach where he gained a little more glory, as his side won the 1950/51 Yorkshire Senior Competition cup. Looking back so far, few will remember that Jim was a household name in his day, but many more will remember him as a local publican, happy to talk Rugby League. Jim was also a key figure in the Castleford RL Players Association, an official in the organisation and a popular guest for many years. His passing was a very sad day indeed for his colleagues.

Jim 'Ginger' Crossley moves in to tackle during a 1935 Challenge match in Lyon, France.

Jim Croston

Centre three-quarter, 1933-1945

Appearances: 283

Tries: 150

Goals: 52

Drop Goals: 0

Points: 554

Previous club: Armed forces rugby union

From serving his country to serving Castleford, the signing of Jim Croston proved to be a shrewd move indeed, as the young recruit went on to give great service to the club and the game. Credit must go to the Castleford chairman, Gideon Shaw, for moving in when the name of Alfred James Croston, a soldier playing for his service's union team, was brought to the club's attention. Cas duly bought Jim out of the Army and signed him on professional forms. He soon made an impact, in fact, sooner than he expected. Croston was sent along to watch Castleford take on Bradford in October 1933, in order to learn a little about the game, but a late withdrawal paved the way for him to be drafted into the starting line-up. Slotted onto the wing, he learnt more quickly than he might have expected had he watched from the terraces and, playing as A.N. Other, the new boy notched a debut try, the first of many. However, he was soon switched to what became his regular position of centre and, alongside Arthur Atkinson, formed what was regarded by many at the time as the best centre partnership in the game. The two of them complimented each other perfectly; Atkinson had the power and strength whilst Jim brought guile and speed. Jim was also a superb tackler, and few were able to beat his deadly spotting. It also seems that he was quite an innovative players. At the time of his arrival at Castleford, shoulder pads didn't exist, but Jim used to have a shin pad strapped to what he called his 'crash shoulder' and he used that to great effect in his tackling.

Atkinson and Croston were, of course the Castleford centres in the historic first Wembley cup final win over Huddersfield in 1935 and, the following year, they were expected to be part of the Great Britain touring party bound for Australia. But, to the surprise of many, only Arthur got the call. Jim did go on to make his GB debut in 1937, playing for Britain in their 5-4 Headingley win against the Aussies, but that was to be his only appearance at that level. However, between 1936 and 1939, Jim won himself 6 caps with England, which gives a better indication of his ability to play with and against the best. He was also the first Castleford player to represent Lancashire, ultimately winning 8 caps for the Red Rose team.

After twelve years at Cas, Jim made the short move to local rivals Wakefield in an

Jim Croston pictured before the Challenge Cup semi-final against Barrow in 1935, which Castleford won 11-5.

Jimmy Croston lines up at Wembley, 1935.

exchange deal for Trinity's Ron Copley, and he went on to give great service to his new club. In fact, eleven years after winning the cup with Castleford, and well into his thirties, he repeated the feat with Wakefield. He was the player/manager at Belle Vue and led his side to a famous Trinity win at Wembley in 1946, and even scored one of their tries. Ironically, although playing for his second Yorkshire club, his final opponents were Wigan – Croston's hometown team. But it was Wakefield who narrowly won the day. Croston was revered at both Castleford and Wakefield – an achievement to which few can lay claim!

Derek Edwards
Full-back, 1960-1972

Appearances: 305(4)

Tries: 38

Goals: 1

Drop Goals: 0

Points: 116

Previous club: Local junior rugby

When Derek Edwards signed for Castleford, it was as a scrum-half; yet he went on to become one of the club's finest ever full-backs. Derek was born in Wheldon Road and, seventeen years later, he was to play at the ground which bore the same name when he signed from the Castleford Juniors in 1960. After a year in the second team, Derek made his senior debut against Doncaster and he was soon showing his potential as a lively half-back. He would almost certainly have had a successful career in that position but, unfortunately for Derek, two guys called Hardisty and Hepworth rightly had a mortgage on those positions. However, when coach George Clinton spotted Derek's potential as a full back, his career really took off. His linking from that position was brilliant and when the ball was kicked in his direction, the broken field in front of him seemed so inviting. In fact, the opposition kicked to Derek Edwards at their peril as, more often than not, the yards gained by the kicker were paid back with interest. That wasn't his only strength because, despite his relatively slight frame, Derek was a tremendous tackler. He won medals in Castleford's three BBC2 Floodlit Competition victories and, in 1968, Derek's form earned a call-up by Great Britain for the World Cup. More

medals came his way in Castleford's 1969 and 1970 Wembley triumphs and also in 1970, when he was one of five Castleford players in the British touring party to Australasia. Altogether, Derek won 5 GB caps and a similar number for Yorkshire.

However, back to 1970, and with cup-winner's medals and international honours, rugby life couldn't have looked much better for Derek and his Cas teammates. But things went rapidly downhill over the next couple of years and, in 1972, Edwards was to become another star to quit Castleford in acrimonious circumstances. He had stayed away from close-season training over a reported problem with his benefit money and, with the club not wanting to transfer him, he announced that he was packing in the game. But, by December, he was to follow Alan Hardisty and Keith Hepworth in a move to Leeds for just £5,000. It was simply a case of economics for Cas. Derek was staying away from the club and hadn't played for eight months, and gates at Wheldon Road were averaging under 2,000, so, as chairman Ron Simpson said: 'I didn't want Edwards to go, but what can you do

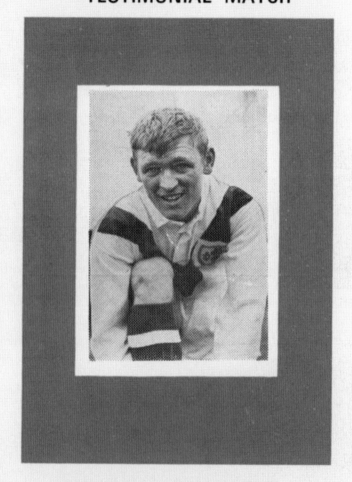

Cas defeated a combined Humberside team in Derek Edwards' 1972 testimonial game.

Derek Edwards almost breaks the tackle in the 1969 Challenge Cup final.

when you only attract poor gates?' All common sense of course, but his words didn't make the fans any happier who, having already lost Malcolm Reilly to Australia, had now seen three more of their club's top players switch to Headingley over an eighteen-month period. However, Derek didn't share the success that Hardisty and Hepworth had with Leeds and, twelve months later, he was on his way to Keighley and from there to Doncaster, where he had a stint as coach. But, whatever the circumstances surrounding Derek's departure, he was another quality player whom, fans felt, had plenty more to offer at the time of the fall-out with Castleford.

From half-back to full-back, Derek Edwards was another local product who made it to the top.

St John Ellis

Wing three-quarter, 1989-1994

Appearances: 173(2)

Tries: 97

Goals: 17

Drop Goals: 0

Points: 422

Previous club: York

When York-born St John Ellis joined the Tigers from his hometown club, few at Castleford knew too much about the flying winger, but by the time he left for Australia five years later, everyone knew who he was. 'Singe' was not just a record-breaking tryscorer he was also a great entertainer. Ellis had impressed Cas officials in a pre-season friendly match when he scored a couple of tries against the Tigers. With the ability to play full-back and centre as well as on the wing, he was seen as a very useful addition to the squad – but he became much more than that. He signed for Castleford in 1989, at a time when coach Darryl Van De Velde was bringing a number of new faces to the club, in a deal rated as £30,000, with Cas paying £20,000 and prop Dean Mountain moving to York.

Having stepped up from the Second Division, Singe was to make his Cas debut against international opposition in the shape of the New Zealand tourists. The Kiwis, who included former Cas player Gary Freeman and future Tigers stars Tawera Nikau and Brendan Tuuta, just snatched victory 22-20, but, for St John Ellis, it was his first real taste of big-time Rugby League. It certainly wasn't his last. Before the end of the season, Singe had firmly established himself in the Cas starting line-up, grabbing 23 touchdowns and making himself a real favourite with his elusive, if somewhat unorthodox, running style. Those tries included a club record-equalling five in a match, as Whitehaven were put to the sword in the Regal Trophy, 62-2. Just a couple of months after joining Castleford, the new boy (still a relative unknown) was writing himself into the record books. The following season saw the bargain buy called up by Great Britain, as Singe made his international bow, coming on as a substitute against France in Perpignan. He added a second cap, again as a sub, in the return clash with the French at Headingley – all of this took place just fifteen months after stepping up into the top flight.

In his third season with Cas, Singe picked up his second Yorkshire Cup winner's medal and come April 1992, he was winging his way to Wembley. Sadly, there was to be no winner's medal this time. The following campaign was a quieter one for both the player and his club, but, in season 1993/94, Singe's last one with the Tigers, he came back with a bang. Castleford were playing some top-class rugby and piling up the points, with St John Ellis right at the heart of the try-scoring action. He scored a hat-trick against the New Zealand tourists, as Cas defeated the Kiwis 16-4, and was scoring tries for fun in the domestic competition. Surprisingly, Singe wasn't amongst the scorers as the Tigers thrashed Wigan to take the Regal Trophy, but three months later, with two tries against Wakefield at Belle Vue, he took his seasonal tally to 38 tries. This impressive total beat the club record of 36, which had been set by Keith Howe twenty years previously. Amongst this club glory, St John was also starring on the international front again, representing Great Britain in the Coca-Cola World Sevens in Sydney and winning a third Test cap against France. But although he was winning honours and breaking records, Singe wasn't happy with

the way contractual negotiations at Cas were going, and he stunned the clubs fans by requesting a transfer. He was 'reluctantly' listed at £200,000. St John added 2 more tries to his tally, finishing the campaign on 40, a record that has never even been threatened since, but they were his last tries for Cas.

Singe got his move, to Australia with his old coach Van de Velde at the Queensland Crushers, but he left many fond memories behind him. Since returning to England, he still lives locally and he is now carving a name for himself in coaching with the Doncaster Dragons. Indeed, his current club is playing with the kind of flair that made their boss the player he was.

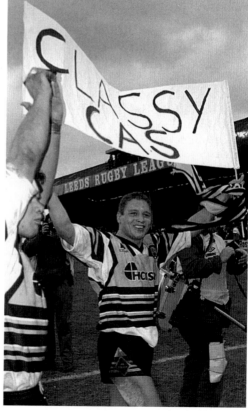

Left: St John Ellis in action in the 1994 Regal Trophy final. *Right:* The Regal Trophy won and it's time to celebrate.

Keith England

Prop/second-row forward, 1981-1994

Appearances: 310(36)

Tries: 33

Goals: 0

Drop Goals: 0

Points: 130

Previous club: Local junior rugby

Keith England, or 'Beefy' as he soon became known, was very much the local hero – one of so many who have figured in the Castleford ranks. Born in the town, he signed for his local club in 1981 having graduated through the academy ranks. Over the next thirteen seasons, Beefy went on to play almost 350 games for the Tigers, always showing the same fierce determination. He was a real 'bread and butter' player of the game. Beefy's style involved few frills but plenty of hard work – an ethos that keen fans identify with and appreciate, but which is not always fully recognised by others.

Thankfully, the right people did appreciate Keith England's efforts as his international recognition (11 Great Britain caps, a GB tour place in 1990, GB Under-24 and Colts caps and a place on the first ever GB Under-18s' tour of Australia in 1982) proves beyond any doubt. And, as for his club, Beefy gave his all when on duty for his country. Couple those personal honours with a clutch of domestic medals for Cas, add the fact that he was always a big crowd favourite who, despite his fame, remained 'one of us', and you have all the ingredients

of the aforementioned local hero.

Beefy made his first-team debut against Workington Town in October 1982 and, by the following April, the nineteen-year-old was beginning to turn his promise into performance as a try-scorer in Castleford's narrow Challenge Cup semi-final defeat against Hull at Elland Road. That was the first of two semi-final defeats that he was to suffer at the hands of the men from west Hull. However, his third semi-final appearance (against Oldham in 1986) was to prove the 'lucky' one, as Cas won and set themselves on the road to Wembley after a sixteen-year gap. In the final, they were to meet the other Humberside outfit, Hull KR. Beefy, as ever, played his full part in Castleford's success at the Twin Towers against Rovers, as he was to do again six year later, scoring one of his side's tries on the Tigers' next Wembley visit. That though was mere consolation for him as Cas, despite a brave effort, failed to halt Wigan's (ultimately record-breaking) run.

However, Beefy isn't short on medals, with few players able to match his seven Yorkshire Cup finals (three winner's medals and four runners-up gongs) through the 1980s and '90s. In fact, few players were more consistent for Castleford over those years but by 1993, his place in the first team was no longer guaranteed. He did add another medal to his collection, playing for the Alliance in the Yorkshire Senior Competition Cup final against York, but at the end of the following year's campaign, he was allowed to go out on loan and he joined Second Division side Rochdale. That loan led to a permanent move and Beefy served the Hornets well in his 66 appearances.

As his time as a professional came to an end, Beefy prolonged his playing career by turning out for both Lock Lane and Redhill, local amateur sides in Castleford, and, in effect, ending up back where he started – in his home town.

'Beefy' at Wembley in 1992, where he was a Tigers try-scorer.

Keith England taking on the Huddersfield hooker at Wheldon Road in 1988.

Mike Ford

Scrum-half, 1991-1994 & 1997-1998

Appearances: 151(12)

Tries: 57

Goals: 8

Drop Goals: 0

Points: 236

Previous club: Oldham (first spell), Wakefield (second spell)

Mike Ford had two spells with Castleford, in very contrasting circumstances, but his contribution to the Tigers cause was massive both times. A former Wigan player who featured in the memorable Wembley final of 1985, Mike found opportunities limited at Central Park and left to join Leigh before moving on to Oldham. He became a key player in the Oldham ranks, but after their relegation in 1991, he asked for a move, hoping to stay in the top bracket and further his international claims. A fee of £150,000 was put on his head, which was later reduced to £95,000, but when the Tigers swooped for his signature, they got their man for £77,500, and that proved a bargain.

In his first season at Cas, Mike won a Yorkshire Cup final winner's medal, as well as a runners-up gong in the 1992 Wembley final, after playing a leading role in Castleford's semi-final victory over Hull. Later that year he got the break that he had been looking for when he joined Cas, with a first international call-up from England for their match with Wales. Mike had won 4 Great Britain Under-21 caps whilst with Wigan and Leigh, but, at twenty-seven, this was his first senior call-up –

just reward for the consistency and quality he was displaying for the Tigers. When the Great Britain selectors announced their squad for the two-match series with France in 1993, Mike was promoted from the England team. He took the field as a second-half substitute in Carcassonne to add a senior British cap to his collection, scoring a debut try for good measure – a feat he repeated in the second match with France, again as a second-half substitute. Mike was revelling in what had become a quality line-up at Castleford, and their tremendous 1994 Regal Trophy win was no more than the team deserved after missing out on the major competitions for eight years. But having failed to make it a double after defeat in the 1994 Premiership final at Old Trafford, Castleford fans were shocked to learn that Mike was set to quit the club and move to Australia. Teammate St John Ellis had already agreed to join his former coach Darryl Van De Velde, who had quit Cas the previous year, at his Queensland Crushers club, and losing another key player in Mike was a massive blow for the Tigers. A fee of £60,000 was reported, but that was small comfort as Castleford's best team for years was starting to break up within weeks of a highly successful season.

Sadly, that break-up continued over the next couple of years, during which time Mike returned to England after a couple of somewhat

A typical Mike Ford break during his second spell with the Tigers.

disappointing years with the Crushers. After a spell with Warrington, he had moved on to Wakefield and was playing at Belle Vue in the Second Division at the same time as his former club, Castleford, were facing the real threat of relegation in their 1997 Super League campaign. However, after stepping into the shoes of John Joyner, caretaker coach Mick Morgan soon realised that there was an urgent need for a playmaker in the Tigers' ranks, and, once again, Cas turned to 'Fordy'. Thankfully, he had a clause in his contract that allowed for him to talk to any Super League club who might come in for him and, whilst the Wildcats

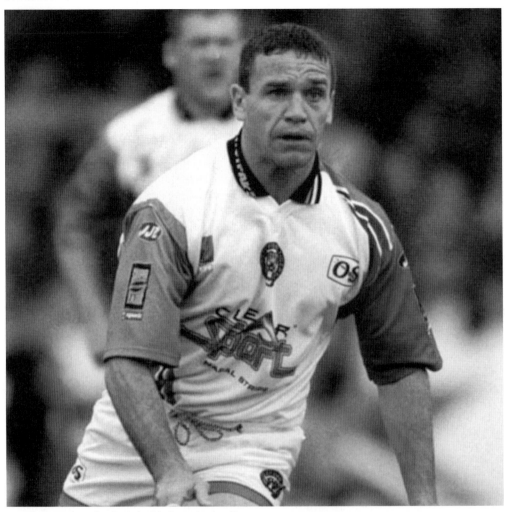

Mike Ford in action for Castleford in Super League III.

didn't like it, Cas took advantage of it and concluded a deal with Wakefield which brought him back to the club. He fulfilled perfectly the role that 'Morgy' saw for him, and along with the injection of other new blood that new boss Stuart Raper had applied, Mike gave the club impetus and enthusiasm that was desperately required, and his role in Castleford's successful fight against relegation cannot be underestimated. Mike was also handed the captain's role at Cas and he was perfect for the job, which he retained in 1998. However, that was his last year at Wheldon Road. Typically, he bowed out with a match-clinching performance in his

last game for the Tigers, against London, and he was given a huge ovation by the Castleford fans. Mike himself said: 'Cas has been like a second home to me and the fans have been superb.' For their part, they were just glad to have had him at their club, especially twice over.

However, at thirty-two, Mike still had plenty of rugby in him and he did a tremendous job back at Oldham as player/coach before moving into Rugby Union with the Irish national team. But his great talent will surely bring him back to Rugby League one day – probably as a successful coach in Super League.

Ronnie Gibbs

Second-row forward, 1988-1989

Appearances: 41

Tries: 12

Goals: 0

Drop Goals: 0

Points: 48

Previous club: Gold Coast Giants (Australia)

Ronnie 'Rambo' Gibbs had two all-too-brief spells with Castleford in seasons 1988/89 and 1989/90, both as an off-season guest from his Australian club. His reputation and nickname, from Sylvester Stallone's film portrayal of a tough, all-action ex-soldier, were already with him, and he lived up to the billing. He was a hero to the Castleford fans, but a villain to their opponents. Ron signed for the club in 1988 from the Gold Coast Giants on a short-term deal and arrived with a reputation as one of Australia's toughest players. But whilst he was undoubtedly rugged and tough, he was a fair player who was badly treated in England on the basis of reputation rather than deed.

Ronnie came to prominence Down Under as a strong-tackling centre with the Eastern Suburbs club before a switch to the illustrious Manly Sea Eagles. At Manly, he switched to the second row and, although he was with the Giants when he joined Cas, it was his time with Manly that paved the way for the move. The year before joining Cas, Ronnie had played alongside Kevin Ward in Manly's Winfield Cup-winning side and it was his wish to team up again with 'Wardy' that made him opt for Castleford when Leeds and Wigan were also chasing him. Perhaps adding to his reputa-

tion, his last match for Manly was in the World Club Championship at Wigan, when he ended that phase of his career with a sending-off. Ronnie's debut for Cas was a try-scoring one against Hull, but two games later he was dismissed against St Helens in an incident that confirmed to Tigers fans the reputation that had preceded him. This was to become a familiar problem, yet Ronnie was far more sinned against than sinning, with more than a few wanting to make their name with a cheap shot on 'Rambo' Gibbs. He collected a runners-up medal in the 1988 Yorkshire Cup final but, more importantly, Ron became a massive favourite with the Castleford fans, who loved him and warmed to his all-action approach and his constant willingness to put his body on the line.

He left for home after that guest spell with the tribute from club's cairman, David Poulter, of being: 'The best overseas player that we have had in my four years as chairman.' There was talk of Ron's return in 1989, but, by this stage, clubs were signing players from overseas on long-term contracts, as the short-term deals started after

Ron Gibbs crosses the line despite the attention of the Leeds defence.

'Rambo' nreaks through the Halifax cover in this 1988 clash.

the UK season kicked off and ended before its finale. Unfortunately, Ron was only available from his Aussie club on a short-term deal. However, his popularity was such that he was brought back anyway. 'The only player we would have brought over on that basis', said Mr Poulter, and Cas fans had the pleasure of a second term of Ronnie Gibbs.

In the interim, he had had another great season with his Aussie club, yet throughout his career Ron was unable to win major representative honours. Possibly those in power felt that his reputation made him a potential liability, but, ironically, some of his big hits would these days have the Sky TV pundits 'Eddie and Stevo' waxing lyrical!

Alan Hardisty

Stand-off half, 1958-1971

Appearances: 400(1)

Tries: 206

Goals: 78

Drop Goals: 42

Points: 858

Previous club: Local junior rugby

Regarded by many as Castleford's finest ever player, Alan was a mercurial stand-off half whose pace and skills could take him, seemingly effortlessly, through the tightest of defences. A brilliant try-scorer and an accomplished kicker, Alan notched over 200 touchdowns for his hometown club as one of only four players to pass the 400-appearance mark for Castleford.

He broke the heart of many a Castleford follower when he joined arch-rivals Leeds in 1971 after a brief spell as player/coach at Cas, but many felt that Alan had been given little chance to prove himself in the coaching role. After the most successful spell in the club's history, the side was going through a period of great transition and 'Chuck', as he was fondly known, left the club amidst some bitterness. It certainly wasn't the way that such a distinguished and loyal player should have parted company with his hometown club, although his own popularity in Castleford has rightly never waned.

Alan's career with Castleford was launched in the late 1950s when the club's fortunes were at a fairly low ebb. His first-team debut came as a seventeen-year-old at Keighley in September 1958, and he was the first of what was to become a wealth of top local youngsters who were given their chance as the club had a shift in its recruitment policy. If anyone was to confirm the wisdom of that change in the system, it was Alan Hardisty. He became a regular in season 1960/61 and, although it wasn't entirely down to Alan, it was no coincidence that the club's rise in stature tied in with his.

His numerous match-winning performances for the club have ensured that his hero status remains to the present day. Those who were fortunate enough to see Alan play will recall that he could appear not to be involved in the match for long periods, only to pull out some magic and clinch victory for his side. Not noted for his tackling, there were others who could fill that role, notably his long-time partner Keith Hepworth, but his mercurial attacking skill were what people paid to see.

Alan was a Great Britain tourist to Australasia in 1966 and 1970 and, in total, won 12 Test match caps and 5 for the Yorkshire County side. His first GB cap was won against France in 1964 and, in another era, more international honours might have come. However, in his greatest years, there was some exceptional half-back talent in

Alan Hardisty recieves the Yorkshire League Trophy in 1965, with long-serving forward Clive Dickinson alongside him.

Alan Hardisty touches down for Castleford's only try in the 1964 Challenge Cup final replay.

the game of Rugby League and Test caps were very hard won.

Alan's finest hours came when he captained Castleford to successive Challenge Cup wins at Wembley against Salford in 1969 and against Wigan in 1970. In 1969, Salford were the big spenders of Rugby League and had recruited far and wide, including some big-money captures from Rugby Union, and were hot favourites to take the Cup. However, the homespun Castleford team had other ideas. The Reds were leading when Malcolm Reilly broke through, and at his shoulder was none other than Alan Hardisty. Alan raced through for the touchdown and, having taken the lead, which they never lost, he led his side to their first Challenge Cup win for thirty-four years.

After leaving his hometown club for Leeds, Alan was back at Wembley in 1972 with the 'Loiners' but, on this occasion, he picked up a runners-up medal, Leeds losing to St Helens. However, over the next two years he completed a full set of winner's gongs in winning Players Competition and Championship medals. It was a shame that they didn't come with Cas, but he deserved to win all that the game offered.

Alan had a spell Down Under after leaving Leeds, with the Rockhampton club in Queensland where he was player and coach, as well as looking after the regional representative side, Central Queensland. It was a short stint though, and the last for Alan as a player. Once back in England, he again got involved in coaching, with spells as head coach with Dewsbury and York. But Alan found another vocation in physiotherapy and that is a skill that he practises to this day with a business back home in Castleford.

Dennis Hartley

Prop forward, 1966-1975

Appearances: 259(9)

Tries: 15

Goals: 1

Drop Goals: 1

Points: 49

Previous club: Hunslet

The Castleford side that earned the tag 'Classy Cas' in the 1960s won a lot of admirers for their open and flowing style of rugby – but they won precious little in the way of silverware. Opponents clearly felt that they had a 'soft centre', which could be outmuscled in big games. But the signing of international prop forward Dennis Hartley was as much as anything the catalyst in taking the club into the big time. A big, tough forward, Dennis was already well established in the game, with Great Britain honours, when Cas paid a fee of around £4,500 to bring him to the club. Those who watched Castleford at the time of his capture would argue to this day that there never was money better spent.

Dennis started his professional career at lowly Doncaster before moving to Hunslet, with the Dons receiving their then record transfer fee. At Hunslet, he was a member of the south Leeds club's pack that took part in an epic Challenge Cup final against Wigan in 1965 – for many, Wembley's finest ever occasion.

In his first two campaigns for Cas, he stiffened up the pack immeasurably and picked up two BBC TV Floodlit competition winner's medals along the way. Very few opponents took liberties with Dennis around, and that was an important factor in allowing fiery young forwards such as Malcolm Reilly and Brian Lockwood to develop their own games and to go on and become world stars. As such, the 'Classy Cas' side added a touch of steel to their play. Leeds, as is the case now, were great rivals and the ferocity of some of the Castleford clashes with their neighbours from Headingley can only be imagined these days. But with Dennis in Castleford's corner, few took a backward step in these clashes. He wasn't a dirty player though – and, in fact, he was a real gent off the field – but he could look after himself and in turn commanded a great deal of respect. He was also a very skilful player. He could be surrounded by opponents attempting to bring him down and still slip the ball out to a team-mate, who then had several fewer players to face!

Whilst with Castleford, Dennis added 9 more Great Britain Test caps to his collection, taking his total to 11. He also made 4 appearances for Yorkshire. Dennis was a tourist to Australia and New Zealand in 1970 – still the last time GB won an Ashes series, some thirty-plus years on – and he

Where are they? Few opponents relished taking on Dennis when he was on the charge.

Dennis Hartley in action against Leeds.

lost nothing in comparison to some big rough-and-ready Aussie forwards. But to the amazement of many well beyond the confines of Castleford, Dennis wasn't in the original tour party. Wigan prop John Stephens dislocated his hip and had to pull out of the squad, but whilst that was cruel luck for him, it enabled the selectors to right a wrong and Dennis was off to pack his cases. In fact, the Cas ace had been unlucky to miss out on the 1966 tour, but, at thirty-three, this would have been his last chance. Typical of the man, he said at the time: 'Whilst this fulfils a great ambition for me, I feel sorry for John. I didn't want a tour place to come to me this way.' But he was a great success, and Dennis has said himself that the tour Down Under was one of the highlights of his career, as were the two successful Wembley trips he made with Cas in 1969 and 1970, when he was the cornerstone of a tremendous pack.

He retired from the game at Castleford a highly respected figure and, as many comment, 'they don't make them like that anymore.' However, he wasn't finished with the club. He joined the coaching staff when his playing days were over and played a major role in developing the early careers of many youngsters who came through the ranks at the club. Indeed, he is still a regular at the Jungle to this day, watching the club he did so much for, both as a player and as a coach.

Keith Hepworth
Scrum-half, 1958-1971

Appearances: 325(4)

Tries: 66

Goals: 4

Drop Goals: 14

Points: 234

Previous club: Local junior rugby

A childhood chum of Alan Hardisty at the Ashton Road school in Castleford, Keith Hepworth became inextricably linked with his schoolmate as they formed Castleford's legendary half-back pairing – the 'H-bombs'. They had thirteen years together at Castleford and it should have been longer, but both left the club in somewhat controversial circumstances to link up again at Leeds and gain more glory. In fact, it is hard to talk about Keith, or 'Heppy' as he became known, without reference to Alan, but they were different characters and ultimately went their separate ways in the game.

The duo signed for Castleford within a week of each other and, although Alan went on to earn more fame and a higher profile, the duo remain Castleford's most famous partnership, and many feel that neither would have achieved as much as they did without each other. For example, Alan Hardisty wasn't noted for his tackling, but Keith Hepworth certainly was, and he seemed to love the task.

Heppy made his Castleford debut in April 1959 at Huddersfield and, although he notched a debut try, it was a losing start to his career. He was to figure in many more defeats before his and Alan Hardisty's influence provided the catalyst for Castleford's rise in fortunes. He also was to produce many lines for the famous BBC commentator Eddie Waring, who took delight in talking about Keith's keen interest in racing pigeons.

Heppy made the first of his 5 appearances for Yorkshire in 1965 and, two years later, he made his first of 11 Great Britain appearances in a Test match with France in Carcassonne. By now, he and 'Chuck' Hardisty were established as one of the game's best half-back partnerships and, for many, the finest in Castleford's history.

When Castleford did hit the big time with their Wembley double in 1969 and 1979, Heppy was inevitably a leading light. He scored the last of Castleford's three tries in their 1969 success, finally killing off Salford, who had pulled back to be just two points in arrears with minutes to go. But when Cas again reached Wembley in 1970, Keith Hepworth, who didn't always get the headlines he deserved, found himself in the news for the wrong reasons. Castleford's opponents were Wigan, whose full-back Colin Tyrer was, at the time, one of the game's finest goal-kickers. At the end of the 1969/70 season, Tyrer was the Rugby League's leading points scorer and, in the opening two minutes at Wembley, he added two more as he converted a penalty to

Keith Hepworth (centre) registers his approval with Alan Hardisty (left) and Bill Bryant (right).

give his side the lead. Cas drew level though, and then took the lead after Alan Lowndes had crossed for the game's only try, but then came the sixteenth-minute incident when Heppy clashed with Tyrer, which led to the Wigan full-back taking no further part in the game. Tyrer was led from the field with blood pouring from a head wound, and the situation wasn't helped when, at half-time, the Wembley scoreboard flashed up the message: 'Tyrer taken to hospital with suspected fractured jaw.' Wigan were furious, claiming that Heppy should have been sent off, with their coach describing the incident as 'diabolical'. In fact, referee Fred Lindop did book Keith, but Tyrer was substituted.

Keith Hepworth was a tough, but by no means a dirty player, and he said afterwards: 'I was committed to the tackle, I didn't do anything deliberately.' But many of the headlines didn't echo his sentiments: 'Tyrer injury a crucial blow to Wigan hopes' in the *Sunday People* was a mild example. Yet when the dust had settled, it transpired that Tyrer had suffered the relatively minor injury of lacerated gums – no

broken jaw – and television replays weren't conclusive. Writing for the *Daily Express*, Jack Bentley, a very distinguished Rugby League journalist, said: 'I could produce a list of players for whom late-tackling actions are not unknown. Keith Hepworth would not be on it. I cannot recall his being involved in a similar incident in all of the hundreds of tackles I have seen this solid little defender make.' It was a fitting statement on the incident.

By the way, Castleford did actually win the cup, but Heppy didn't have too long to dwell on the victory as he was one of five Castleford players selected for the Great Britain squad to tour Australia and New Zealand – a measure of the club's status at the time. The exploits of that 1970 GB party live on to this day, with no subsequent group coming close to matching them, and Heppy was, inevitably, at the helm. He played in the three Tests against Australia, when Britain last took the Ashes, and two of the three against the Kiwis, which brought the tourists another series win.

However, there were rumblings of discontent. At the beginning of the 1970/71 season,

Hepworth asked Castleford for a transfer. No reason was made known, but his request was granted and he was put on offer with a £12,000 price tag. There was a World Cup taking place at the same time, and Heppy retained his Great Britain place for the tournament. However, the Aussies gained revenge for their Ashes defeat just months earlier, defeating Britain 12-7 in the final. There was better news for Castleford, as Heppy came off the transfer list, but it was to prove only temporary. Just before Christmas, he again asked to go on the list, and again Castleford complied. For some reason, in three months his value had dropped so that he was now on offer at £8,000. Cas hoped that they were on the way to a third successive Wembley appearance though, and Heppy was in the side that took them through to the semi-final against Leeds. However, injury ruled him out of that match, which Cas lost, and the club eventually lost Heppy.

His partner, Alan Hardisty, had left the club to join Leeds, in circumstances that had left Cas fans nonplussed, and it was no surprise when Heppy joined him at Headingley. He cost Leeds just £4,000 and, much to the fans' chagrin, two of Castleford's finest ever players found themselves plying their trade at the home of one of their biggest rivals. The duo went on to prove that they still had plenty to offer, as they achieved a great deal of success at Leeds. Heppy spent five years with the Loiners, but that wasn't the end as he had a stint with Hull before concluding his playing days. What a pity that they didn't take place at his hometown club.

Keith Hepworth gets a pass away against Leeds.

Barry Johnson

Prop forward, 1979-1988

Appearances: 206(16)

Tries: 22

Goals: 1

Drop Goals: 0

Points: 67

Previous club: Local junior rugby

Barry Johnson was one of the most gifted young ball-handling props of his time, and it was a tragedy that didn't achieve as much in the game as his skills deserved. Unfortunately, Barry had bad luck with injury, especially when his ability made him a target for some individuals who weren't fit to lace his boots in terms of playing ability.

Barry was amongst a clutch of top youngsters to join Cas in 1979, with most going on to achieve success, him being one of the first. By the end of the 1980/81 season, he was a regular in the first team, and in the early part of the following campaign, he won the Man of the Match award as Castleford defeated Bradford in the Yorkshire Cup final. 'Immaculate ball distribution' was just one of many comments made about Barry's performance. His ball skills were out of the top drawer for someone so young, one match report in a 1981 Castleford programme describing how 'Barry Johnson fooled the entire Warrington defence before sending Robert Beardmore over'. At the beginning of 1982, at just twenty-two, Barry was appointed as the Castleford skipper and, just two weeks later, he was also given the hon-

our of captaining the Great Britain Under-24 side to victory over France at Headingley. Barry retained his place for the return match in Tonneins, which brought another win for his young Lions, and he looked set to lead his Cas side to Wembley before a narrow 11-15 semi-final defeat at the hands of Hull.

Barry started the new 1982/83 campaign in top form – 'the man with the most expressive pair of hands in the game' was how Jack Bentley described him in the *Sunday Express* – and full Great Britain selection seemed just a matter of time. But again it was heartache for Barry and his men as Hull put them out of the Challenge Cup at the semi-final stage. Despite that defeat, things were going well for Barry, but it was all so different the following season when, on the opening day of the campaign, he suffered a broken jaw in a match at Featherstone. Rugby is a tough game, as everyone who watches and plays it is only too well aware, but in the modern parlance, Barry took a 'cheap shot' that afternoon at Post Office Road. It was, as the subsequent Cas programme called it, 'a sickening injury', and few that were at the match would have argued with that description. The injury kept Barry out of action for four months, but three matches into his comeback, his jaw was broken again, in exactly the same place, and his future in the game was thrown into doubt. Specialists advised that Barry should pack the game in and he too asked the question whether he should come back 'just to be a target'. It was an understandable reaction with his season decimated and now at an end; a season in which he might confidently have expected to have won a place in the 1984 Great Britain tour party.

Thankfully, Barry didn't call it a day, but there are those who felt that his career was thereafter affected by the injuries that were inflicted upon him in that season. In addition, he had again to overcome the disappointment of a Challenge Cup semi-final defeat, by Hull, for the third time in four years. But Barry was to be rewarded for fighting back and for perseverance when he was in the Castleford side that bridged a six-teen-year gap in reaching the 1986 Challenge Cup final at Wembley. He was part of a Cas pack that laid the foundations for the victory over Hull KR, and there can't have been a happier man in London that afternoon. Five months later, a 1986 Yorkshire Cup winner's medal followed, but an operation to rebuild his shoulder muscles decimated the 1987/88 season for Barry. When he couldn't command a regular first-team place the following season, it was no surprise when he decided to move. Ambitious Bramley paid a club record fee for Barry and that was to spell the end of his top-flight career, although he has continued to work in the game, including doing some radio broadcasting with some well thought-out comment. He was a quality player though, who ultimately got his rewards, but he should have had more.

Barry Johnson takes on Halifax hooker Seamus McCallion in 1987.

53

Appearances: 585(28)

Tries: 185

Goals: 0

Drop Goals: 0

Points: 614

Previous club: Local junior rugby

John Joyner was also the Castleford coach from 1993 to 1997.

John Joyner was one of Castleford's finest players and the holder of a record that may never be broken: that of over 600 appearances for the Tigers. Castleford was Joyner's only club, with whom he spent twenty-five years as both a player and a coach. Joyner was actually born in Leeds, but had long since moved to Cas when he signed for the club back in February 1972. He was signed to play with the club's Under-17 side, but, at seventeen, he made his first-team debut when Castleford defeated Bramley 18-0 in November 1972. John made a further 11 appearances that season, but by the following campaign, he had established himself as a regular, and that remained the case until his retirement as a player at the end of the 1991/92 season. In the 1992 close season, another chapter in Joyner's career with Castleford opened up when he was appointed assistant to the then coach, Darryl Van De Velde.

However, that was only at the end of a highly illustrious playing career, during which John won a string of honours, including becoming only the third Castleford player to lift the Challenge Cup at Wembley. In his very first season at the club, he won medals with

the 'A' team as they completed a League and Cup double, but he saw very little of the 'second team' after that. As a classy centre, he was a key member of the 1976/77 Castleford side which won silverware in the Players and the Floodlit competitions and, in that same season, John made his international debut for the Great Britain Under-24 team which defeated France. The following season brought him a first Yorkshire Cup winner's medal and two more GB Under-24 caps, but the following year was to bring John his greatest honour. The Australians were touring England, and after they had defeated GB in the first Test, home coach Peter Fox rang the changes – John Joyner, still in his early twenties, was one of the new faces, and made a winning debut as Britain levelled the series. John's international career was to span ten years, ending after his third Lions tour in 1988. During that time, he made 16 Test appearances as well as playing 20 other matches for GB on tour. He also represented England 4 times, GB Under-24's on 5 occasions, and Yorkshire 12 times, giving him a remarkable representative total of 57 appearances.

On the club front, Joyner evolved from centre to stand-off to loose forward with ease, showing equal ability whatever his role. He won further Yorkshire Cup medals and remains the last Cas skipper to hold aloft the Challenge

John Joyner in action in the 1981 Yorkshire Cup final against Bradford Northern.

Cup. He won many matches for his side but one quote best sums up 'JJ' as a player. It wasn't a big match and it was one of numerous plaudits he received throughout his career, but it says it all. The author was then *Yorkshire Evening Post* writer Trevor Watson when, after an top-class Cas performance in defeating Leeds in 1986, Watson observed: 'When Joyner blinked a gap appeared in the Leeds ranks. If he cleared his throat, there was chaos.'

Now back to that second chapter in Joyner's time with the Tigers. As the 1992/93 season drew to a close, the popular Aussie boss Van de Velde announced that he was returning home to take up a post with the Queensland Crushers and the search was on for a new boss to fill his shoes. A number of Van de Velde's fellow countrymen applied for the post, but the Tigers board decided upon promotion from within – Joyner was handed the reins. As a coach, Joyner

led the Tigers to one of their greatest ever successes when they trounced the star-studded Wigan side 33-2 in the 1994 Regal Trophy final, the biggest defeat the Warriors had ever suffered in 87 major finals. In a memorable season, John also took his side to the semi-final of the Challenge Cup, where Wigan exacted some revenge with a 20-6 win, and to the Premiership final at Old Trafford. Here Wigan were to gain further revenge for that Regal Trophy defeat, but not before Castleford had pushed them all the way, only to finally slip 20-24. It was no surprise though when Joyner, in only his first year in the job, was named the 1993/94 Coach of the Year, beating off competition from John Dorahy at Wigan and one Gary Hetherington. The current Leeds Rhinos chief executive, Hetherington, was then coach at Sheffield Eagles and a former team-mate of John's in the Castleford juniors.

After two finals, one semi-final and fourth position in the League, things were looking good at Castleford but, as had been the case in the past at such times, things started to go wrong. Former coach Van de Velde tempted two of his former charges and two of the club's biggest stars, St John Ellis and Mike Ford, to join him in Australia and their replacements weren't of the same calibre. But nevertheless, whilst not having the same cup success, Joyner lifted his side to third in the table. However, a home defeat to Warrington ended their Premiership hopes, and after losing two stars at the end of his first season in charge, Joyner was to suffer a similar fate in his second, as Kiwi aces Ritchie Blackmore and Tony Kemp quit for Auckland and Leeds respectively. In the close season, he was hit with another blow as promising youngster Andy Hay was allowed to leave the club. Understandably, Joyner was reported to be 'unhappy' that top name players were leaving the club and not being replaced. He was pleased though to be appointed as assistant coach to England boss Phil Larder, but his Tigers side was sliding. New signings weren't successfully replacing those departing stars and, by the end of the inaugural Super League campaign of 1996, Cas were down to ninth in the table, closing the season with a 0-56 defeat at London – the writing was on the wall.

However, Joyner's departure, after twenty-five years at Castleford, came in disappointing circumstances. A surprise home defeat to Salford ended any Challenge Cup hopes at the first stage, before Joyner lost yet another of his top players when Tony Smith asked to move and was quickly snapped up by Wigan. The team was playing badly and, after the opening 4 Super League matches were lost, a change became almost inevitable. On 3 April 1997, John Joyner's time at Castleford ended with what was described as a 'mutually agreed' parting of the ways. It was a sad day for both parties, but John remains very much a Cas 'great'.

Jubilant coach John Joyner celebrates Castleford's 1994 Regal Trophy win with celebrity Michael Parkinson (left) and director Eddie Ashton.

Appearances: 43

Tries: 3

Goals: 0

Drop Goals: 1

Points: 11

Previous club: Halifax

Cumbrian second-row forward Bill Kirkbride played in just 43 matches for Castleford during a two-year spell with the club, but one of those matches was as big as they come and he played a major role in it. Bill signed for the club from Halifax in 1969 for the sum of around £6,000 – a tidy sum at the time – but the rangy back-rower who had moved to Halifax from Workington Town soon made his mark at the club. He slotted into a pack that had already tasted Wembley success earlier that year and added another dimension to an already strong forward line-up. Within weeks of signing, he was adding to his County honours with selection for Cumbria, but Bill's finest hour was to come when Cas defended the Challenge Cup in 1970.

They reached the Wembley final again after an impressive campaign, with Bill's one and only drop goal for the club being one of the three that saw off St Helens in the semi-final at Swinton. Better still was to come in the final against Wigan, as Castleford retained the trophy with Bill topping the votes for the Man of the Match award and clinching the coveted Lance Todd trophy. It surely couldn't get much better for the new boy, winning the game's top club and individual honours in under a year.

Yet his stay with the club wasn't a long one though, and before 1970 was out Bill was one of a number of Castleford players to be transfer-listed as the club went through a period of some turmoil. Bill still lived in Halifax, and in the days when full-timers were still a long way off, it was said that a new job was hindering his travelling to and from Castleford and this was possibly the reason for his transfer-listing. However, although a fee of £8,000 was put on his head, he didn't stay on the list too long before Salford snapped him up for £6,500, after barely sixteen months at Wheldon Road.

After a spell with Salford, Bill found himself back in West Yorkshire at Wakefield, initially as a player and then as a coach. He made a return visit to Wembley in that capacity when Wakefield reached the final, but there was no fairy-tale ending this time, as Widnes took the cup.

Bill Kirkbride picks up another award.

George Langfield
Scrum-half, 1945-1952

Appearances: 228

Tries: 62

Goals: 370

Drop Goals: 21

Points: 968

Previous club: Local junior rugby

A local Castleford man, the story goes that George Langfield breezed into the Wheldon Road ground towards the end of 1945, asked for a trial and, a few weeks later, made his first-team debut for Castleford. An outstanding scrum-half and a prolific points scorer, George went on to be the star of his era at the club. Within a couple of years, George's career really took off when he made the first of his 4 appearances for Yorkshire, playing for the White Rose side which scored a tremendous victory over the 1948 Australian tourists.

Season 1948/49 also saw Castleford reach their first ever Yorkshire Cup final and George was, of course, in the line-up. He notched a drop goal, but he and his team-mates had to settle for runners-up medals as Bradford took the Cup with an 18-9 victory. Two years later, George and Castleford made their second County final, but again it was to end in defeat, this time at the hands of Huddersfield. Castleford had done well to reach those finals, but for the ambitious player, the club were struggling in the League.

George played his last match for Cas at Wakefield on Christmas Day before being transferred to St Helens. At the time, Castleford were entering a period that brought very slim pickings and George was understandably looking to better himself, and he was soon chasing honours with Saints. In his first full season at St Helens, he broke the club's goal-kicking record and his tremendous long-range drop goal in the 1953 Challenge Cup semi-final took Saints to Wembley, and a meeting with Huddersfield. However, just as with Castleford in those Yorkshire Cup finals, George was to end up with a runners-up medal, despite a personal tally of a try and two goals.

George added to his Yorkshire appearances whilst at St Helens, but never got further than winning an England reserve spot on the international front. He has nonetheless been a star either side of the Pennines and one of Castleford's best ever half-backs – and there have been many very good ones with whom to compare him.

One of Castleford's greatest scrum-halves, George Langfield.

George Lewis
Full-back, 1929-1944

Appearances: 373

Tries: 19

Goals: 373

Drop Goals: 11

Points: 825

Previous club: Local junior rugby

A local boy who made good, George Lewis actually attended the Wheldon Road School so it wasn't too far for the youngster to travel when he joined Castleford. The full back made his debut against local rivals Leeds at Headingley in 1929, but he can't have been too happy with his first outing as the Loiners triumphed by 40 points to 2. However, it was the first of over 350 appearances for the boy from 'down the lane', who made the last line of defence position his very own over a period of fifteen years. George was a relatively light-weight character, but his tackling has been described as 'copybook' and he was also highly capable in dealing with 'up and unders' – the high balls that were put his way. George was also a first-class goal-kicker, who would have achieved a much higher total than the impressive 373 that he did record, were it not for the fact that during the early part of his career, Arthur Atkinson took many of his side's kicks. When he did take on the goal-kicking role, he was regularly Castleford's leading scorer in the season – a feat he achieved in five campaigns from 1934/35 to 1938/39, with a best of 213 points in the 1935/36 term, when he kicked 99 goals.

George was a player who missed few games. In fact, he might have been looking to make over 500 appearances for Castleford but, like many others, the war years affected his career and, between 1939 and 1945, he played in just 14 matches for Castleford. George was also unlucky to be playing at a time when there were many top-class players filling the same role and, as a result, he was unlucky to miss out on representative honours. However, he did win personal honours as a member of Castleford's first cup-winning side in 1935. George played a big part in taking his club to their first Wembley final, kicking goals throughout the cup trail, although the job went back to Arthur Atkinson for the final itself. There were no more cups to come George's way, although he was also one of the unlucky Cas thirteen who took part in the 1939 Championship final and were narrowly defeated by Salford at Maine Road.

George was also there when Castleford proved to be early pacesetters for European rugby. These days, many might think it a new phenomenon for clubs to play in France but this is not so – Castleford made the trip in 1935 and George was a member

George Lewis in action at Wheldon Road.

George Lewis (middle) lines up between two Aussie tourists before the Cas versus Australia game in 1933.

of the team that faced the Lyons-Villeurbanne team at the Stade Buffalo Velodrome in Paris. The match followed Castleford's Wembley triumph when the club were invited to France, one of the first to cross the channel following the intro-duction of Rugby League into that country just a year earlier. Castleford won the match by 24 points to 21, with a couple of goals to George's name.

George played his last match for Castleford at Hunslet in October 1944, but his full-back role for Castleford was kept very much in the Lewis family. Younger brother Ronnie stepped into George's shoes, and he went on to make 260 appear-ances for Castleford. Although Ronnie joined the club at a time when they weren't in a position for him to emulate his elder brother's feat of playing in major finals, he did collect runners-up medals as a member of Castleford's Yorkshire Cup finals teams in 1948 and 1950. However, Ronnie did manage to pick up the representative honours that eluded George, although it was just the one appearance for Yorkshire, against Cumberland in 1950.

One similarity in the brothers' careers came in 1945, when Castleford again travelled to France. The thirteen-a-side game had been banned in occupied France during the Second World War, but when the victory over Germany was won, it was back to business, and Cas, with Ronnie at full-back for both matches, were invited to undertake a brief two-match tour. The Tigers travelled to play Cote Basque in Bayonne and then to Bordeaux, with the matches bringing a win and a draw.

Great Castleford servants and pioneers as well, the Lewis borthers made impressive contributions to the club's cause with a combined twenty-four seasons.

Bob Lindner

Loose forward, 1986-1988

Appearances: 19

Tries: 9

Goals: 0

Drop Goals: 0

Points: 36

Previous club: Wynum Manley (first spell),
Parramatta (second spell)

Bob Lindner will be regarded by many as a strange choice for this book of Cas 'greats'. The big Aussie had just two brief guest stints with Castleford, didn't always show his best and left in acrimonious circumstances. But he was a very high quality world-class player, showing at times all the skill and ability that had made him a huge star in Australia.

Lindner's signing in 1986, at a time when the English and Aussie seasons didn't run parallel, allowing for 'guest' stints rather than permanent moves, was regarded as a massive coup. At the time of his signing, he was playing in the Brisbane competition, before the Broncos, and although it was seen as secondary to the Big League in Sydney, Lindner was considered a certainty for the 1986 Australian tour of England. He was indeed selected, but the downside for Castleford was that he couldn't take up his contract until the tour was over. Cas fans couldn't wait for his arrival after having seen him in opposition to Great Britain when he scored a try in each of the three Test matches and made some devastating performances. His debut came against Bradford on 1 January 1987 and Lindner was everything that was expected of him – he was a class act.

Lindner was to play just 8 more matches for Castleford before having to return home for the Aussie season where, having switched from Brisbane to Sydney, he linked up with Parramatta.

But before the year was out, he was back at Wheldon Road, again on a short-term contract, this time a little earlier in the season. 'He is a world-class player and we are delighted he has decided to rejoin us', Cas chairman David Poulter said. He was back with a bang. 'Lindner added a touch of class as he ran majestically' was one journalist's description after Cas had put Halifax out of the Yorkshire Cup. However, in the final of that competition, Bob was to suffer a facial injury and from thereon things went downhill. The injury ruled him out for a number of weeks and, when he returned, his form wasn't of the high standard that he had set previously. He was beset by an ankle problem, which was eventually diagnosed as a stress fracture, and it would have kept him out of action for over a month, by which time he would almost have been due to return home. So it was agreed that Bob would cut short his stay and return to Australia for treatment. It was a blow, but fans had appreciated his outstanding skills, albeit only briefly, and wished him well. However, on returning home, Lindner reportedly slagged off the Castleford coach Dave Sampson, which

Former Cas players representing Australia in 1990. From left to right: Bob Lindner, Gary Belcher and Chris Johns.

brought a stinging retort from chairman David Poulter, who branded Lindner a 'disgrace'.

It seems that Bob hadn't bonded too well with the team in his second stint, but the club had planned to keep quiet on the matter until his alleged comments surfaced. Whatever the truth of the matter, it was a sad end to a spell which had promised so very much. And it was a shock as the Aussie imports coming to Castleford generally settled well and spoke highly of the club.

Lindner did return to Wheldon Road, as a member of the 1990 Australian tour party that defeated Cas 28-8, and towards the end of his playing career, Lindner returned to England with Oldham, playing 30 matches in 1993/94. He was on the bench for Oldham in their match at Cas that campaign, but it was a losing return to his first English 'home' as the Roughyed's crashed 34-16. But whilst his team were struggling, Bob still had plenty of ability. His substitution was inspired, if not enough to save his side, but the *Yorkshire Evening Post* reports said it all: 'Lindner transformed Oldham, running strongly up front and stopping anyone who came near him.' Later in the season, when Cas completed a double over Oldham, it was despite a try and 'an heroic performance by skipper Bob Lindner'.

But his real recognition, which provides irrefutable evidence of the player's undoubted ability, was won back home in Australia. Bob made 23 appearances for his native Queensland in State of Origin and he also made 23 appearances for Australia, including tours to the UK in 1986 and 1990 and the 1992 World Cup and none of those honours come cheaply. Just imagine if he'd settled in Castleford in 1988 and signed a long-term deal with the Tigers!

65

Geoff Lloyd —————————————————————————
Back-row forward, 1969-1978

Appearances: 209(16)

Tries: 44

Goals: 741

Drop Goals: 2

Points: 1,616

Previous club: Local junior rugby

Geoff 'Sammy' Lloyd joined Castleford from Fryston juniors as a promising local youngster, making his first-team debut in the 1969/70 season. The following term, he was largely confined to the 'A' team, but as his season wound to a close, a talent was uncovered. Amongst some programme notes when Cas played Hull KR early in 1971, there was an interesting piece that read: 'Geoff Lloyd has surprised everyone recently with his goal-kicking for the 'A' team. In his first two matches as kicker he has kicked 14 out of 16 attempts and really looks a first-class kicker.' How right those words were to prove. 'Sammy' was still finding it hard to break into the first team though, and it was a full year from him finding his kicking boots until he had the chance to demonstrate his skill with the seniors. His chance came against Salford, when his five goals and a try played a big part in Castleford's victory. He came into the side in the second row, although at the time, when everyone was fit, there were players who were probably better in that position. But such were Lloyd's kicking skills that, in those early years, he was often slotted into the side on the wing, primarily as a kicker.

He really made his mark though, when Castleford were drawn at home to Cumberland amateur side Millom in the first round of the 1973 Players No. 6 competition. It was never going to be a giant-killing display from the Cumbrians, as Cas showed no mercy to record a massive 88-5 victory. Leading the way was Sammy Lloyd, now firmly established in the second row, who scored 3 tries and 17 goals to record (in the days of the 3-point try) 43 points. The goals and points totals were both club records, and both stand to this day, with his kicking being almost perfect. Lloyd kicked the first 13 in succession, with the total of 17 coming from just 18 attempts. By the end of that season, he had set a new club record of 121 goals and the following year he again passed the century mark with 112. With 260 points, he was third in the game's leading scorers list.

In the 1975/76 season, Sammy was again kicking goals 'for fun' and broke his own club record, this time with 149 successes. The following term was much the same, with Lloyd kicking some vital cup goals as Cas enjoyed trophy-winning successes in both the Floodlit and the Player's competitions. Once again, he broke his own club record, kicking a tremendous 158 goals – the third 'Sammy' Lloyd record that stands to this day. To round off a marvellous season, although something

Geoff 'Sammy' Lloyd was an excellent goal-kicker and set many records for Cas.

of a surprise, he gained selection for the 1977 Great Britain touring party to Australia and New Zealand. 'I can't believe it,' Lloyd said at the time. 'It looks as though I will have to cancel my holiday in Rhyl.'

More success came in 1977 when Castleford won the Yorkshire Cup for the first time in their history, with five Lloyd goals in the final. With an end-of-season tally of over 100 yet again, Albert Lunn's club record career goals total was well within his sights. But there was a shock in store during the off-season when Lloyd asked for a transfer, saying that he wasn't producing his best form.

Castleford granted his request and put a price tag of £19,500 on his head. When he signed for Hull a month later, the actual fee was reported to be £13,000 for the twenty-six-year-old, and Albert's record was intact.

Having set new records at Castleford, Sammy Lloyd went on to do the same for Hull and his 178 goals and 369 points in 1978/79 still remain records. Five club records that have stood the test of time: proof indeed of a great goal kicker, and an often-underestimated player.

Brian Lockwood

Prop/second-row forward, 1965-1975

Appearances: 221(10)

Tries: 38

Goals: 8

Drop Goals: 0

Points: 130

Previous club: Local junior rugby

Like many of his team-mates at the time, Brian Lockwood was a top prospect as a youngster having made his mark in Castleford schools and juniors rugby. With a host of honours in an outstanding career, there is no doubt that Brian fulfilled that promise to the full, but Castleford fans will feel that it was a great pity that more of his many medals didn't come whilst wearing their side's jersey. That isn't to say that he didn't do well with his local club. He was a Wembley winner with Castleford in their 1969 and 1970 successes and he won representative honours for Yorkshire (at one point captaining the White Rose side), England and Great Britain whilst at Wheldon Road.

During his time at the club, he was a key member of the pack, developing into one of the game's best forwards of his era. Brian had skill in abundance, but he was also a tough character, and those attributes made him an integral part of what was the last GB team to win the Rugby League World Cup. That feat was achieved in France in 1972, when a mere 4,231 people gathered in Lyon to see the British boys, including Lockwood, triumph.

Not surprisingly therefore, there was some concern amongst the Castleford faithful when, in 1974, at a time when their side's pack strength wasn't at its strongest, Lockwood was allowed to sample life in Australia. At the time, the British season took place in the winter and Brian was one of many players who, moving in either direction, spent their own club's off-season playing on the other side of the world. He joined the Canterbury club and enjoyed six tremendous and successful months, with the Bulldogs reaching the Grand Final. The Aussie outfit wanted Brian to sign a long-term deal, but he had promised to come back to Cas in return for the club allowing him this stint Down Under, and just a few hours after jetting in, he was back in a Castleford jersey. Such was his standing in the game that he was selected for Yorkshire just days later and he played a major role for his club, but Brian had enjoyed his time and liked the life in Australia. However, although Brian himself says he didn't push for a move, at the end of the season, Castleford accepted a fee, reported to be £10,000, for his services and he was once again Aussie-bound – this time on a two-year contract. But Brian didn't return to the Bulldogs, instead opting for the Balmain Tigers, with Easts and Penrith also interested.

After two years at Balmain, Brian returned to the UK, but this time it wasn't to Castleford. He took a player-coach role with neighbours Wakefield Trinity, but that wasn't in any way to signal the winding down of his playing career. He left Wakefield for Hull KR and, such was his form, that he was recalled to the GB team, captained England and, in 1980, won the Lance Todd Trophy at Wembley as the Rovers defeated their Humberside rivals Hull to take the cup. But he was soon on the move and, after a short stint with Oldham, Brian moved to Widnes. More glory was to follow as he won a further cup-winner's medal, as the Cheshire side, one of the game's elite at the time, defeated his former club, Hull KR, at Wembley in 1981. In doing so, Brian matched Alex Murphy's record of 4 Wembley appearances with three clubs. Brian almost completed a memorable hat-trick as his Widnes side again reached the final in 1982, but this time they were denied, although only after a replay against Hull at Elland Road after a drawn final in London.

Since leaving the game, Brian has made his mark in the licensed trade at a number of local pubs. He is currently 'in situ' a couple of miles out of Cas, where customers can enjoy a great meal and a look at much of Brian's memorabilia from his playing days that decorates the walls.

Brian Lockwood in action during the 1970 Challenge Cup final.

A typical surge from Brian Lockwood as he looks to hand off another defender against Bradford Northern.

Alan Lowndes

Wing three-quarter, 1968-1977

Appearances: 201

Tries: 83

Goals: 0

Drop Goals: 0

Points: 249

Previous club: Wakefield Rugby Union

Castleford haven't signed too many players from the higher echelons of Rugby Union over the years, but a notable exception was in 1968, when Wakefield RUFC winger Alan Lowndes joined the club. Wakefield were regarded as one of the top teams of the day, certainly in the north, and, in addition to that, Lowndes was a Yorkshire player in the fifteen-man code. Alan had also represented England Schools in the long jump, the 100 yards and the 220 yards events in athletics, so he was quite a capture. However, he made the transition to League look easy, so much so that, in his first season, he won a call-up for the England Under-24 team to play France in April 1969, and he grabbed himself an international debut try into the bargain. In October that same year, Alan made his first Yorkshire appearance, against Cumbria, but although it was to be his only appearance for the County side, he again scored a debut try, which completed a double at that level in League and Union. Days after playing for Yorkshire, Alan was selected for the full England side to play Wales, but sadly an injury meant he had to withdraw and he was never to have another opportunity.

Amidst all of this representative recognition, Alan had also capped his first season

in Rugby League with a Challenge Cup winner's medal, making 1969 a rather special first full year in League. But his greatest moment of glory was yet to come – although he nearly wasn't there to claim it. Cas had battled to a second successive Wembley in 1970, but the week before the big day, they had to face St Helens in the Championship semi-final. Perhaps mindful of the fact that the Castleford players might have had Wigan and Wembley at the back of their mind, the Saints took no prisoners. Most Cas players took knocks in the match, but three, including Alan Lowndes (a hip injury), were injured. The match was drawn, with the farcical situation of the replay scheduled to take place two days after the first match and five days before the game's showpiece final. Castleford, not surprisingly, requested a postponement until after Wembley, but the Rugby League rejected their request. The upshot of that decision was that they sent their entire reserve side to St Helens for the replay and, although defeated, those thirteen youngsters put up a very creditable performance.

Whilst all this was taking place, Alan

Alan Lownes crosses the line for a try against Leeds in 1973.

Lowndes was having daily treatment for his injury and was only just walking easily with three days to go to the final. As the side departed for London, the *Yorkshire Evening Post* reported: 'An infra-red lamp, a battery heater and an electric blanket were vital pieces of equipment on the Castleford coach as they left for their pre-cup final headquarters at Crystal Palace. The items are vital for treatment to winger Alan Lowndes in the race to get him fit for the final.' It might sound a little primitive now, but they did the trick and Lowndes was fit to play his part – and what a key part it was. The final was deadlocked at 2-2 when the game's only try was scored. One flash of inspiration was all that it needed. Thankfully, it came from Cas when Alan Hardisty and Ian Stenton sent Lowndes sweeping in at the corner. He scored over 80 tries for Cas in his career, but none were so sweet nor important as that one.

Alan was out injured for a large chunk of the 1970/71 season but was back the following year, earning a runners-up medal in Castleford's Yorkshire Cup final defeat at the hands of Hull KR. He scored tries consistently throughout the 1972/73 campaign, helping Castleford to another Challenge Cup semi-final, but that ended in disappointment as local rivals Featherstone recorded a comfortable victory to progress to Wembley. The following season he was the club's leading tryscorer, but Alan's career at Castleford was gradually winding down. He scored his last tries for the club in the 1976/77 season before leaving the club. But he was a match-winner at Wembley and that is something very special to look back upon.

Appearances: 363

Tries: 40

Goals: 875

Drop Goals: 0

Points: 1,870

Previous club: Local junior rugby

Albert Lunn was a tremendously loyal player for Castleford whose entire career at the club was during one of the leanest periods in their history. He didn't win honours, despite never giving anything but his best, yet he set two records that still stand almost thirty years on from his retirement.

Albert joined Cas from the Airedale ARL club in 1951 as a goal-kicking full-back, and he went on to make both of those roles his own. His first-team debut in March 1952 was against Belle Vue Rangers, a side from Manchester now long gone. Ronnie Lewis was a solid full-back for Cas and Albert came in at centre for his debut, but it wasn't long before he was playing in his favoured position.

He soon assumed the goal-kicking role and became one of the League's deadliest marksmen. On four occasions he topped the century mark of goals for the season, and this at a time when Castleford didn't often make big scores. At the end of his career, Albert had kicked 870 goals for Castleford and had notched 1870 points – those two records that stand today. His last match came in the Challenge Cup against Leeds in February 1963 when, after weeks of frozen and icy conditions, Castleford were one of the first clubs to get their ground playable. However, it took over sixty braziers burning brightly to thaw the surface, not to mention the efforts of dozens of staff and supporters. The conditions were far from great though, and there was no reward for Castleford's efforts. Albert kicked his last goal for the club, but Leeds won the match 10-8 – Cas were out of the cup and, as the freeze continued, out of action for a further month. The braziers had done their job, but unfortunately they had left the pitch without grass! For Albert, it was his last outing on the pitch as a player, as he heeded medical advice and retired from the game

When Albert retired as a player, he became the groundsman at Wheldon Road and, despite those problems of the 1963 winter, his pitch, as it is today, was always in tiptop condition. Sadly, Albert passed away at the early age of fifty-seven, but the packed church at his funeral service was proof of the tremendous respect that he had earned in the town.

An early shot of Albert, a loyal Castleford man.

Tony Marchant

Centre three-quarter, 1981-1989 & 1995

Appearances: 262(6)

Tries: 101

Goals: 0

Drop Goals: 0

Points: 386

Previous club: Local junior rugby

Castleford must hold a strong influence over Tony Marchant as the Tigers' current senior academy coach is in his third separate stint at the Jungle. He joined the club from the Colts set-up in 1981 as a very promising centre, who was winning representative honours from a very early age. Before he was twenty, he had been in the Yorkshire and the Great Britain Colts sides in the 1981/82 season and, at the end of that campaign, he was selected for the Great Britain Colts squad which toured Australia and Papua. During that same season, Tony was already beginning to make his mark in the first team at Castleford; so much so, that by the following year, when he was still just twenty years of age, he was a regular, making 36 appearances and notching 16 tries.

It was then that he had his first taste of the big time at club level as a member of Castleford's defeated Challenge Cup semi-final side. There were more big-match disappointments to come his way in the 1983 Yorkshire Cup final, the 1984 Premiership final and the 1985 Challenge Cup semi-final, as time after time in that period, Castleford came so near to winning silverware. But Tony and his side were to ultimately find themselves lifting trophies, finally hitting the jackpot in 1986.

However, before that came along, Tony was rewarded with his first Great Britain Test cap when he played and scored a debut try against

France at Wigan in March 1986. Just three weeks after that match, he was to score a far more valuable try – the last of Castleford's three to finish off Oldham in the Challenge Cup semi-final in a victory which took the Tigers to their first Wembley final in sixteen years. It had been Castleford's fourth semi-final in five years and, after three defeats at the hands of Hull, the relief amongst Castleford fans, players and officials was immense – not least because the club was experiencing some financial problems at the time. But now all thoughts were on the cup final and, when the big day came, it was another vital touchdown to Tony Marchant that set Castleford on the road to success. 'Marchant's try was brilliantly taken', wrote Trevor Watson in the *Yorkshire Evening Post*, adding: 'He never put a foot wrong with swift direct running and his tackling was, as ever, spot on.' Some praise indeed, but it was well deserved as the town, which had been hit hard on the industrial front, prepared to celebrate through the summer.

However, for Tony there was to be no off-season, as he jetted out to Australia for a guest stint with top Brisbane outfit Wynum-Manly. In Brisbane, Tony played alongside Ian French, who had guested with Cas during the season and

Tony Marchant shows off the Challenge Cup.

1988, and almost inevitably scored a try in the White Rose win. However, under their new coach Darryl Van De Velde, the Castleford side was going through something of a makeover as the Aussie sought to put his own stamp on things and, midway through the 1989/90 season, Tony was on the move. Bradford Northern was his destination, with the deal reportedly giving Cas a £35,000 fee and young back-rower Neil Roebuck in a cash-plus-player deal.

In 1994, Tony moved on from Bradford to Dewsbury but, a year later, he was briefly back at Wheldon Road, to assist with the coaching of the Alliance side. However, he was called into action on the playing front too, adding his experience to the side with another 9 appearances for the Tigers, as well as scoring the tries that took him past the century mark for Cas. That was the last we were to see of Tony as a player but, after adding to his coaching experience, latterly with Hunslet, Tony was once again to return 'home' in 2002 in that academy coaching role. Still as enthusiastic as ever, Tony came through the ranks at Castleford to grow into a top-quality player. Now his job is to develop a few more to follow in those footsteps and become the players of the future for the Tigers.

had played a significant role in their cup-winning campaign, not to mention the legendary Wally Lewis. It hadn't been a bad six months for Tony – a Test debut, a cup-winner's medal and playing in Australia – but, in the days before full-time professionals, he returned to England and went back to work at the local colliery! However, he was soon to pick up another medal, as Cas defeated Hull in a thrilling 1986 Yorkshire Cup final. He then made a try-scoring debut for the Yorkshire County side. To add to what had already been a dream year, Tony was chosen for the British Test side to face Australia in the first and second Tests. Unfortunately, the Aussies flogged Britain in both Tests, and Tony was one of the many casualties for the third Test, which also went the way of the touring Kangaroos.

The following season, Tony continued his habit of scoring in big matches, with touchdowns for Yorkshire in their War of the Roses clash with Lancashire and again when the County side played the touring Papua New Guinea team. He was unlucky though not to win back an international place, but he was again called up by Yorkshire for his fourth cap when they played Lancashire in September

Tony Marchant in action in 1987.

Roger Millward
Half-back, 1964-1966

Appearances: 34(6)

Tries: 16

Goals: 35

Drop Goals: 0

Points: 118

Previous club: Local junior rugby

Roger Millward was one of the finest Rugby League players ever to come out of the town of Castleford, yet for the most part his talent was used on behalf of the city of Kingston upon Hull. Roger was a star long before signing professionally for his hometown club of Castleford; in fact, he was a television star. At the time (in 1964), ITV was featuring inter-town junior rugby matches and Castleford were one of the best in the competition. Roger had played for the town's Under-17 side since the age of fourteen and, by the time the television company took an interest, he was the side's sixteen-year-old captain and star. Quite simply, the young half-back was the outstanding player in the competition, scoring three tries in the final at Headingley when Cas defeated Widnes, and he captivated both the commentator and the viewers alike.

It was inevitable that he would turn professional, and he did so at Castleford, the team he had supported since he was a youngster. Roger was only small – around 5ft 4in – but he made up for his lack of inches with an abundance of skill, and he wasted no time in showing it after signing for Cas in September 1964. His television appearances ensured that his debut in the second team attracted a crowd of over 1,000 and he let no one down. So well did he

perform, that more than double that number witnessed his next outing. His first-team debut soon followed, and representative honours came almost as quickly. Roger was selected for the Great Britain Under-24 side at just eighteen years of age and, amazingly, he was a reserve for the full GB side just a year after turning professional. In March 1965, when he was still only eighteen and not even a regular in the Castleford side, Roger made his first appearance for Great Britain. He didn't make any further representative appearances whilst at Cas but, by the time Roger had retired from playing, he has amassed a massive 29 caps for Britain and 13 for England.

Unfortunately, for Castleford fans, the reason why Roger was playing for Britain whilst still not a club regular can be put down to two factors – Alan Hardisty and Keith Hepworth. Good as he was, he couldn't displace these two legends from the starting line-up. He was getting into the Castleford team when either was injured, including the 1965 BBC Floodlit competition final, and he had even been used on the wing, but his talent wasn't used to best effect

'Roger the dodger', a local lad whose talent was lost to Humberside.

Roger Millward in action for England against Australia.

there. The bottom line was that Roger was probably the third-best half-back in England, but his team also had the best two.

In 1966, Hull KR reasoned that Castleford might be prepared to sell one of their star half-backs and enquired about signing Roger or Alan Hardisty. Cas fans were very relieved when that bid was rejected, reasoning that the club ought to be able to keep all three happy by whatever means it took. However, shortly afterwards, the club, seemingly reckoning that three into two won't go, had a change of heart, and Rovers got the bargain of the century when they signed Roger for just £6,000. Although it was a long time ago, the fee was nowhere near a record for the game, which, at the time, stood at £11,000. Whether Castleford could have hung onto

Roger is a matter purely for speculation, but many people felt that he would have had plenty of opportunities to play at Cas. In any event, four years later, when Roger was still only in his early twenties, Hardisty and Hepworth both quit Cas for Leeds.

At Hull KR, as both a player and later as coach, Roger was a tremendous success. He captained and coached his side to Wembley finals and also led them to Premiership honours in a stay of twenty-five years with the Humberside club. He scored over 200 tries for Rovers, kicked hundreds of goals and is rightly afforded legendary status in Hull and, for his international exploits, in the game of Rugby League. For Castleford, it is simply a case of what might have been.

Appearances: 164(1)

Tries: 25

Goals: 0

Drop Goals: 0

Points: 100

Previous club: York

It was testimony to his popularity that when Tawera Nikau played his last match in England, for Warrington against Castleford in 2001, both sets of supporters gave the Kiwi a standing ovation. Indeed, of all the many fine overseas players that have donned a Castleford jersey, one of the very best was New Zealander Nikau. He was a tremendous acquisition for the Tigers and, in his five years at the club, he never let his standards slip. When Darryl Van De Velde brought Tawera to the club in 1991, it was a real coup, because it was in the face of competition from around the globe. Auckland in New Zealand and the Canterbury Bulldogs in Australia (to name but two) wanted him on board and, from nearer to home, Leeds and Halifax were also reportedly chasing his signature. Yet at the time, Tawera was playing in the Second Division with York, albeit that they were a stronger Wasps outfit than the their fans have enjoyed in recent years.

Tawera first came to the attention of English fans as a member of the 1989 Kiwi tourists. He didn't make the Test side on that tour, but he did well for the midweek team, including playing a match at Wheldon Road

for his country against Cas, and his displays alerted clubs in the UK to his talent. The Sheffield Eagles stepped in to sign Tawera and his Kiwi colleague Francis Leota from the Otahuhu club in New Zealand, and the two Kiwis immediately made a big impression. However, he played just 10 matches for the Eagles and, at the end of the campaign, he was snapped up by the ambitious York, who had ended their season fourth in the table. With the Wasps, Tawera, who by this time had graduated to Test football, only enhanced his growing reputation. But York again failed to climb any higher than fourth in the table, and by now there was a clamour from much bigger clubs for the signature of Tawera Nikau.

But despite that worldwide interest, it was Castleford who won the day, with Tawera signing on a three-year deal, and saying: 'It is a very good deal, but I didn't just go there for the money. I want to win things and I think that Castleford are the side to do it with.' He didn't have long to wait. Tawera made a winning debut for the Tigers, with almost 9,000 people at Wheldon Road to watch Cas topple Wigan 38-26. Just a couple of months into the season, he was collecting his first silverware with his new club as Castleford took the Yorkshire Cup, defeating Bradford 28-6. The new boy had the honour of being made captain of his side when injury forced

Lee Crooks' late withdrawal. More glory was soon to follow in what was turning into an incredible first season for the Kiwi. A Man of the Match performance from Tawera took his Tigers side past Featherstone in the Challenge Cup quarter-final, and it was he who started the move for the semi-final's only try, as Cas beat Hull 7-2. From York to Wembley in twelve months! Unfortunately, it was the wrong result against Wigan in the final, but Tawera loved it at Castleford and the fans loved him.

There were no cup finals for Cas the following season but, in Tawera's third campaign at the club (1993/94), he made two – again it was won one, lost one. He started the season playing at Wembley again – this time for New Zealand against Great Britain. However, he was omitted from the Kiwis' side for the second and third Tests, and it was back to business on the club front. He was Man of the Match in the second and third rounds of the Regal Trophy, and he was simply magnificent in the semi-final win over Bradford. On the eve of the final against Wigan, Tawera boosted Castleford's hopes when he signed a two-year extension to his contract with the club. He boosted them still further by opening the Tigers' scoring in that Regal Trophy final and setting them on their way to a memorable and famous victory. Wigan took revenge in the Challenge Cup semi-final though, and again in

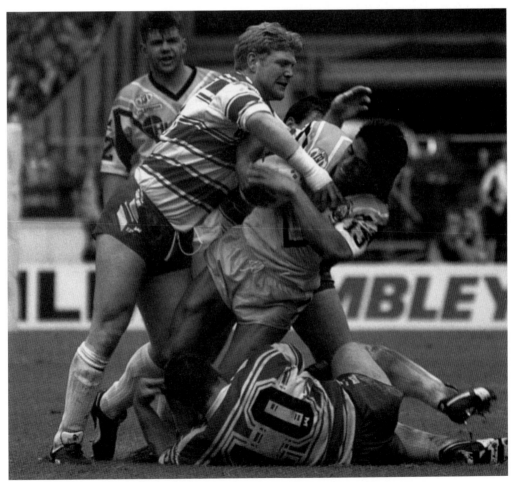

Wigan's Neil Cowie and Andy Platt tackle Tawera Nikau in the 1992 Challenge Cup final.

Tawera Nikau takes on Wigan's Kelvin Skerrett at Wembley, 1992.

the Championship final, but it had been another memorable campaign for Tawera.

It was probably his best ever season for the club as, during those additional two years he had signed up for, they went through a great deal of change. Sadly, a Tigers side somewhat on the slide couldn't hold on to Tawera. His last match for the club came against St Helens in the fourth round of the 1996 Challenge Cup, and his Castleford side crashed out, 16-58. He had enjoyed a short summer stint with the Cronulla Sharks in 1995 and returned to the club in 1996, at the end of his contract with Cas. He was a big star in Sydney, but when the newly formed Melbourne Storm were casting around for talent, they hooked that big star in Tawera and he headed south. The Storm made an immediate impression Down Under, with much of their success put down to the former Tiger. Melbourne were the 1999 NRL Premiers, and Tawera was fêted, but he shocked the game when he announced a return to England, rejoining his former coach at Cas, Darryl Van De Velde, who was now holding the reins at Warrington. He spent two years with the Wolves and, despite being in a side that struggled at times, his own class shone through, reminding fans in England once again what a top player Tawera Nikau was.

Steve Norton

Loose forward, 1969-1977

Appearances: 170(13)

Tries: 56

Goals: 4

Drop Goals: 1

Points: 177

Previous club: Local junior rugby

When a local player of real class emerges, the hope for a club like Castleford is that he will spend his entire career with them. Sadly, in the case of Steve 'Knocker' Norton, that wasn't to be the case, and, after developing at Castleford, it was, in the main, Hull FC who benefited from his outstanding skills. 'Knocker', as he soon became known, graduated through the junior set-up at Castleford and signed for his hometown club in 1969. Just one year later, after only a handful of first-team appearances, the seventeen-year-old was named by coach Tommy Smales as substitute for Castleford's trip to Wembley to face Wigan. The youngster wasn't called from the bench that afternoon, but he more than made amends with a string of big-match appearances over the years.

Signed as a loose forward, 'Knocker' switched to the centre position and made his first appearance in a final in 1971, when Castleford were defeated by Hull KR in the Yorkshire Cup. The next season saw his first senior representative call-up, when he made his debut for Yorkshire in the County Championship. Back in the loose-forward position the follow season, Knocker was out of action for a while with back problems. Although he was regarded as one of the game's most promising young stars, it was still

a surprise when he was called up for the Great Britain tour to Australia and New Zealand in the summer of 1974. He made his Test-match debut against the Kiwis on that tour, the first of 23 international caps, and his career took off from there. More County call-ups came later that year, and when the England squad for the 1975 World Championship was named, it was no surprise to see Steve Norton's name included. He played in all of England's matches in the Australian section of the Championships, and was again called up by his country when the tournament resumed on home soil later that year.

Season 1976/77 was a very good one for the Castleford club, with trophies collected in both the BBC TV Floodlit competition and the Players No. 6 competition. Injury ruled Knocker out of action until the semi-final stage of both competitions, but he made a big impression when he did play. The Floodlit final was against Leigh, and Knocker hit the headlines for the wrong reasons when he was dismissed in the thirty-second minute after a clash with Dave Chisnall, someone who was himself no stranger to controversy. At the time Castleford trailed 0-1, but Knocker's team-mates overcame his dismissal to win the match. A month later, minnows Blackpool gave Cas a scare in the Players final, but their class prevailed and, on this occasion, Knocker lasted the full eighty minutes to collect his second winner's medal of the season.

That was to be the last happy moment for Knocker at Castleford, though, as things were to turn sour before the year was out. In the summer of 1977, he spent his second spell guesting with the Manly club in Australia and they were reportedly keen for him to stay. After his return, he had niggling injury problems and didn't play for Castleford at the start of the campaign, before stunning the club with a transfer request. His request was granted, and Knocker found himself on the market at, what was at the time, a staggering £25,000. That didn't deter a number of bidders, and Cas accepted player-plus-cash offers from both Wakefield and Leeds, only for the player to be unable to agree terms with these clubs. Always a character, both on and off the field, he agreed to join Leeds at one point, only to have a change of heart and, at twenty-five years of age, announce his retirement! However, in January 1978, Hull stepped in with an offer of a five-figure fee, plus their GB Under-24 international forward Jimmy Crampton, and Castleford accepted. For what was classed as a world record transfer deal, Steve Norton left the club he had joined some nine years earlier.

At Hull, he went on to become something of a folk hero, appearing in a string of cup and Premiership finals, as well as adding to his international appearances. Jimmy Crampton's career at Castleford was blighted by back problems and, although he had the ability, he made little impression.

Steve Norton in action against Leeds in the early 1970s.

Steve Norton in action for England.

Appearances: 126(23)

Tries: 51

Goals: 258

Drop Goals: 3

Points: 723

Previous club: Local junior rugby

(Statistics to end of May 2002)

Danny Orr has said many times since that, as a youngster, his ambition was to play for Castleford. When he joined the club from Kippax ARL, he achieved that ambition, and he capped it in 2002 when he was appointed the club's skipper, which made him, at just twenty-three, the youngest captain in Super League at that time. However, with many years ahead of him, Danny has the ability to set himself plenty more goals, and to achieve them.

After switching from Kippax, the young half-back continued his development through the Castleford academy set-up where, for a time, he played under his father Paul, himself a former Cas player, who was then part of the Tigers' coaching team. In season 1995/96, Danny was a member of the Tigers' academy championship-winning side and, a year later, he was further honoured at that level when he captained the Great Britain academy side to victory over their French counterparts. Perhaps disappointingly, very few of that outstanding Castleford academy side have gone on to achieve real success in the game.

Danny's first-team debut came in Castleford in 1997 and it was a baptism of fire,

as his club were fighting against relegation, but he survived it with flying colours and, injuries permitting, he hasn't been out of the Tigers' side since. In those early appearances, coach Stuart Raper occasionally used Danny in the hooking role, but he is a half-back, in either of the two positions, and that is where he is at his best. In 1998, at the end of Danny's second year in the first team, he won the Back of the Year award at the Cas presentation evening. By the start of the 1999 season, people outside Castleford were really starting to sit up and take notice of the Tigers' young star. 'Danny Orr was the quicksilver inspiration behind the impressive win over Hull,' wrote Robert Mills in the *Evening Post*. 'Danny Orr's emergence as one of the game's outstanding young stars was underlined with another eye-catching display', the *Pontefract & Castleford Express* told its readers – the season was just two weeks old! But there was heartache to come for the young protégé when, after kicking a drop goal in the dying minutes of the Tigers' Challenge Cup semi-final tie with London to level the scores and set up extra time, the Broncos grabbed a winner in the last move of the match. It was an early lesson of how cruel the game can be at the highest level. But Danny didn't let that defeat affect his form and, as he approached his twenty-first birthday, he won a place in

Danny Orr looking for an opening against Widnes, 2002.

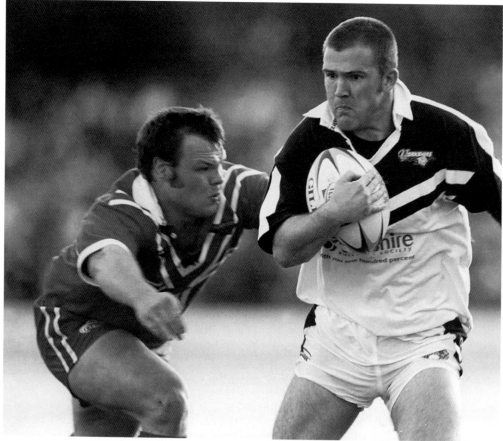

Danny Orr in action for Yorkshire at Headingley, 2001.

the Great Britain training squad that was preparing for the end-of-season tour Down Under. Unfortunately, Danny narrowly missed out on selection for the tour party to Australia, but he had the consolation of making his England debut, scoring two tries as France were defeated in Carcassonne. He also kept his place for the return match at Hull, when he was one of five Tigers on international duty.

After another strong season in 2000, Danny was very unlucky to miss out on a place in the England squad that contested the World Cup but, in 2001, the introduction of the Origin Roses game gave him a Yorkshire County debut. He turned in an impressive performance against Lancashire, until one of the Red Rose pack decided that Danny would be

better out of the action! That turned out to be the case for most of the rest of the season as a result of the injury he sustained in that match.

But Danny was back in the Yorkshire side for the 2002 series, and he was back to his best for the Tigers. He was again on stand-by for Great Britain, but didn't get the call. However, he remains one of the brightest young stars in the game and is the man that Cas fans hope will lead their side back into serious contention for the major honours. It's a big responsibility, but Danny seems to thrive on that, and if he can fulfil his own ambitions at Castleford, then it's safe to say that the Tigers will have real success once again.

David Plange
Wing three-quarter, 1985-1991

Appearances: 191(2)

Tries: 98

Goals: 5

Drop Goals: 0

Points: 402

Previous club: Doncaster

When Castleford brought in a trialist winger from the then lowly Doncaster club in 1985, it didn't exactly send their fans' pulses racing, but David Plange went on to prove that he could do just that. David was a confident, exciting young player, and he made the transition from 'Donny' to the First Division look easy, which quickly made him a big fans' favourite at Wheldon Road. He immediately became a first-team regular, and it was no surprise when Cas turned his trial into a permanent signing in a cash-plus-player exchange deal that took Mark Roache to Doncaster. Dave himself had joined Doncaster from Rugby Union; having played for Scunthorpe and won a County call up in the fifteen-a-side code for the Combined Nottinghamshire, Lincolnshire and Derbyshire side. However, he had played League as a youngster, representing Hull Schoolboys in the 1976 Wembley curtain-raiser. Ten years after that match, barely a year after joining Castleford, David was back playing under the famous Twin Towers. This time though, it wasn't as a schoolboy, but as a strapping, strong twenty-year-old winger. Of course, he walked away from Wembley as a winner, as he did again five months later in the 1986 Yorkshire Cup final, in a season which saw David top the Castleford scoring charts, notching 21 tries.

Cas again reached the Yorkshire Cup final in 1987, and David's 'fearless drive for the corner' to score a try was typical of his determined approach, but the match ended all square and Bradford took the replay. Despite that disappointment, it was all smiles for David just three months later as Great Britain called him up for the first time. 'It's a big surprise, but it's a big chance and I aim to take it', said Plange. And he did just that, scoring one of Britain's tries as they defeated France. However, it wasn't enough to win David a place on the end-of-season Lions tour, and it will have been of little comfort to him to be named in the stand-by squad. In 1988, Cas reached the Yorkshire Cup final once again, but it was another disappointment for David and his side as Leeds thwarted them in front of a massive 23,000 crowd at Elland Road. However, there was some consolation a couple of weeks later when he played for Great Britain against the Rest of the World.

That second was to be his last appearance for his country, but David continued to be a prolific scorer for Castleford and,

Another try for David as he crosses the Hunslet line.

after missing the start of the 1990/91 campaign, he made his first appearance of the season in the Yorkshire Cup final and produced a match-winning performance. Cas were hot favourites against Wakefield, but their local rivals gave them a fright and, were it not for a magnificent tackle by Dave, they would have built a 10-point lead. As it was, the scoreline stayed at 8-4 in Wakefield's favour before David's sixty-third minute touchdown, converted by Lee Crooks, proved a winner.

Plangey was also a scorer for Castleford against the Aussie tourists, but it was the winger on the Tigers' other flank, St John Ellis, who won the international calls that season. It was to prove David's last season with Castleford. After being left out towards the end of the previous campaign, David stayed away from the club during the build up to the 1991/92 season, and it was perhaps no surprise when coach Darryl Van

De Velde agreed a swop deal with Sheffield. Plangey moved to the Don Valley with Dave Nelson coming to Cas in exchange.

But David remained a prolific try-scorer with the Eagles, and more so with his next club, Hull KR, with over 60 tries in a couple of years on Humberside. David's next move took him to Hunslet, where he played and ultimately coached – a role in which he has established a strong reputation. So much so, that, in 2002, he was given his first Super League appointment when Warrington put him in charge. A real character as a player, David inevitably shows a more serious side as a coach, but he has the same will to win that he had as a player, and that should ensure success for whichever team he is associated with.

Appearances: 344

Tries: 70

Goals: 0

Drop Goals: 0

Points: 210

Previous club: Local junior rugby

Ken Pye was another of those Castleford players who might well have won honours had he been with the club at a more successful time in its history, or had he been at a more successful club. Yet he gains top marks for loyalty, having made almost 350 appearances for his local side. Pye was a very versatile player – whilst many centres graduate to the back row later in their careers (and these days scrum-halves and hookers appear almost interchangeable), Ken moved from scrum half to prop forward!

Ken was signed from local junior side Half Acres in 1950 as a scrum-half, and it was in that position that he made his first-team debut a year later, against the long-since defunct Belle Vue Rangers. Cas were struggling around the foot of the table (as they were to do for much of this era) and it was a less than memorable debut for Ken as his side crashed 5-39 to the Rangers. Despite his own endeavours and consistency, this was to be the story of his career with Castleford, with the light at the end of the tunnel only beginning to appear for Cas as his career was drawing to a close. His early career was as the club's regular scrum-half, but as his figure to became less svelte, the prop-forward role seemed more suitable. Apart from the odd game in other positions, his career at Cas was split roughly 50/50 between shirts number seven and number ten.

He missed very few matches for his club in either role and, during his time at half-back, he notched his share of tries, with 13 in 1953/54 making him the club's leading scorer that campaign.

Ken's last game for Castleford came in 1962 and, unlike his first, it was a winning result, as Hunslet were defeated 22-12. He left to join Keighley, largely unsung in the game, but nonetheless a Castleford stalwart who is remembered with some fondness.

Ken's bother, Jos Pye, also played for Castleford. He joined Castleford a year after Ken in 1951, spending six years at the club and playing in 79 matches.

Ken Pye in his prop-forward years at Castleford – another loyal servant to the club.

Stuart Raper

Head coach, 1997-2001

Appearances: 0

Tries: 0

Goals: 0

Drop Goals: 0

Points: 0

Previous club: Cronulla Sharks (Australia)

Stuart Raper was the Castleford coach from 1997 to May 2001.

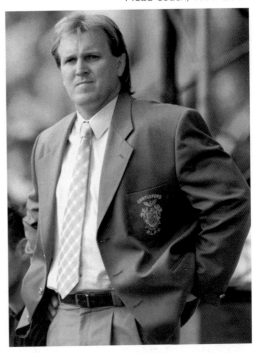

Although he never played a match for Castleford, former coach Stuart Raper could go down as one of the club's most influential figures ever. Raper didn't actually win anything with the Tigers, but he is widely regarded as saving the club from relegation to the Northern Ford Premiership – in effect, the game's second division – in 1997, which could have been a disaster for the club. At the time, some in the game felt that Super League was going to develop into a big city league – with little room for small town clubs, regardless of their achievements and past history. Had Castleford suffered relegation, there would have been no guarantee that they would ever return to the top flight.

The Tigers made a very disappointing start to the season and, after losing their first four matches, the club and coach John Joyner parted company. Enter Stuart Raper. Another four games had been lost following Joyner's departure, and the picture was looking grim by the time the Aussie landed at Castleford. Raper's father John was a legend in Australia. He had been a Test player of the highest calibre and, although son Stuart had played the game Down Under as well as having a brief spell in the UK with Oldham, he hadn't been able to match his father's feats on the field of play. However, he was making his mark as a very promising coach – 'the best young coach in Australia' said his chief executive at Cronulla, Shane Richardson.

He later said that he hadn't realised how big the task at Castleford was, but he tackled it and succeeded. The Tigers' first two matches under his control were lost, but the first win that season came in a thrilling home victory over Salford, with the scenes at the Jungle at the sound of the hooter being akin to winning at Wembley. The battle was on. Further points were won in hard-fought battles, but the dogged Tigers responded to Raper's prompting and, at the end of the campaign, finished above both Paris Saint Germain and Oldham, just a couple of points away from bottom spot.

The Tigers built upon this very narrow escape and, in 1998, climbed to sixth in the table. The 1999 season was another big year for Raper and his Castleford side though. The Tigers reached the semi-final of the Challenge Cup, only to be defeated in the last minute by London after a thriller, regarded by many as the best game at this stage for years. At the same time, they were rocking the so-called big boys in the League. Wigan were defeated twice, whilst the Tigers were unlucky

The Raper brothers – Alan (left) and Stuart (right) – celebrate as defeated Leeds coach Graham Murray looks on.

to gain only draws against Leeds and Bradford. However, at the end of the regular season, they had clinched fifth place in the League and a play-off place. They travelled again to Wigan – the first rugby match to be played at their new JJB Stadium – and Cas defeated the Warriors for the third time that year. The next round brought a trip to Headingley, where 17,000 saw the Tigers pull off a victory that stunned Leeds. Sadly, as in the cup, the semi-final proved a bridge too far for Raper's men, as they crashed to defeat against Saints. However, under the Aussie boss they had taken just two seasons to go from almost certain relegation to being eighty minutes away from the Grand Final.

The following campaign, Raper again led his men to the play-offs, but this time there was no progress beyond the first stage. It was possibly time for a change but, nevertheless, it was a disappointment when Wigan moved in for Stuart midway through 2001. But he had done a tremendous job for the Tigers, who didn't stand in his way, and he won the respect of the Warriors faithful when he guided his new side to Challenge Cup success within twelve months of taking over.

Stuart Raper also brought his brother, Aaron, to Castleford in 1999. The former Parramatta Eel and Australian international hooker spent three seasons with the Tigers and, although injury blighted the latter stages of his time at the club, he was inspirational during that first campaign.

Mick Redfearn

Prop/second-row forward, 1965-1977

Appearances: 291(29)

Tries: 26

Goals: 387

Drop Goals: 8

Points: 868

Previous club: Local junior rugby

Mick Redfearn joined Castleford as a centre from the club's junior side in 1964, and made his debut at just seventeen years of age. He switched into the second row and then moved up to the prop-forward position, gaining a reputation as a solid, hard-working player. However, when, in an emergency, Mick took on the goal-kicking role, he added a string to his bow that was going to bring him greater fame.

As the statistics show, Mick kicked many goals for Castleford, but none were as priceless as the five that he kicked at Headingley on 29 March 1969, for they were the ones that took his Castleford side to Wembley for the the first time in thirty-four years and only the second time in the club's history. Opponents Wakefield had matched Castleford's tally of two tries and their goal-kicker was the legendary Neil Fox, but, on the day, he couldn't match the dead-shot Mick, who kicked his five goals from just five attempts, including one from the touch-line and one from fifty yards. As Mick had also kicked three goals for Cas in their 9-5 quarter-final triumph over Leeds, with each side scoring just the one try, his part in Castleford's march to Wembley had, to say the least, been a very significant one. In the final, goal-kicking chances were tough, but he did grab himself a cup final goal. A year later, he went on to add a couple more Wembley goals, when Cas retained the trophy with a 7-2 victory over Wigan.

Mick made just the one representative appearance, playing for England Under-24's against France in April 1969, in a match that took place at Wheldon Road. The England youngsters recorded an emphatic 42-2 victory, with four Mick Redfearn goals included in their tally. However, that was to be his only international call.

Towards the end of his time with Castleford, Mick wasn't figuring too much in the first team, and, in 1977, he was transferred to Huddersfield. His career at Cas certainly wasn't just those five semi-final goals – but for those alone he deserves to be remembered.

Mick Redfearn shows off his goal-kicking technique.

Malcolm Reilly

Loose forward, 1967-1971 & 1974-1986

Appearances: 294(22)

Tries: 68

Goals: 9

Drop Goals: 4

Points: 230

Previous club: Local junior rugby

Another legendary figure in Castleford's history, Malcolm Reilly OBE, went on to become a major playing and then coaching star in both England and Australia. Malcolm's entry into the game of Rugby League has become established in Castleford folklore, coming as it did because a soccer match was postponed. The young Malcolm Reilly played Rugby League at school, but he had developed quite a talent with the round ball. However, one winter afternoon in 1966 changed things around. The football and rugby teams from Kippax Welfare were preparing for their afternoon's matches, but the soccer match, which Malcolm as a regular was set to play in, was called off because of the bad weather. However the rugby boys decided they could play, and, rather than face an afternoon of inactivity, Malcolm joined them. That was the start of a glorious career in the game of Rugby League.

Castleford scouts soon spotted the potential of the young Reilly, and he was invited for trials. After just two outings with the second team, he signed on the dotted line. The powerful youngster, who joined Cas as a centre but soon switched to loose forward, soon made a big impression with his fearless style. In his first season, he won the first of many medals, in the BBC TV Floodlit competition. Before too long though, bigger and better honours were to come his way. Castleford hadn't been to Wembley for thirty-four years, but when they reached the Challenge Cup final in 1969, the stage was set for Malcolm to produce a masterly performance, which brought his side a victory over glamour side Salford, and brought him the Lance Todd Trophy award as Man of the Match. Castleford's future looked to be set, despite being unlucky to miss out on a League and cup double when Leeds pipped them in the Championship final. They cruised through to another Wembley final in 1970 and, en route to that final, Malcolm learnt that he had been selected for the 1970 Great Britain touring party to visit Australia and New Zealand. The 1970 final was a tight affair, and few knew that Malcolm had been ill on the eve of the match, but he played his usual game and his team once again lifted the Challenge Cup after defeating Wigan.

The Australian tour brought Malcolm onto the world stage in Great Britain's Ashes-winning side and he revelled in the spotlight. He proved an inspiration for his country in all three Tests against the Aussies, and the people Down Under certainly liked what they saw of the young British lock. Unfortunately, for Castleford fans, that feeling was reciprocated. There was a World Cup competition in England later in 1970, and Malcolm was again at the helm of the GB efforts, but the Aussies had their revenge for the Ashes defeat by winning the competition. At club level, Castleford were hoping for a third Wembley appearance, but before their semi-final defeat, Malcolm Reilly was on his way to play club rugby in Australia. The Aussie glamour team, the Manly Sea Eagles, had agreed to pay Cas a then world record transfer fee of £15,000 and, although Malcolm was a more precious commodity than the cash, he was keen to try his luck in the Sydney Big League.

It was no surprise to anyone at Cas that he became a big hit on the other side of the world and, in a highly successful spell with Manly, he won back-to-back Grand Final winner's medals in 1972 and 1973, to add to his Challenge Cup medals.

However, Malcolm was back in Cas by 1974 and played for his hometown team in the 1974/75 season, ironically, for the local boy, as a 'guest' on loan. His first game back at Wheldon Road added 800 to the attendance from the previous match, but it was still a meagre 2,600. These were fairly thin times for the club, but Malcolm was impressive; scoring a try as Cas beat Halifax 35-10. Shortly after Malcolm's return, the Castleford coach, Dave Cox, left the club to work in Australia and, in a move that both shocked and delighted the Castleford fans, Malcolm was appointed as the club's new player-coach. As a loan player with the club, he had to return to Australia to fulfil his commitments to Manly, but he was to return to the UK for the 1975/76 season as the fully-fledged Cas boss.

An ongoing knee injury restricted Mal as a player but, within a couple of years, he had rebuilt the Cas side and, in 1976/77, he led them to success in the finals of the BBC2

A typical Malcolm Reilly move as he collects one of his own kicks to score.

Supporters hold Malcolm Reilly aloft after Castleford's 1986 Challenge Cup semi-final victory over Oldham.

Floodlit Competition and the Player's Trophy. The following season, still defying his injury, Malcolm captained and coached Cas to their first ever Yorkshire Cup final victory. The inspirational player was becoming an inspirational coach. However, his playing days were becoming less frequent, although he could still show his ability in key matches. Again, a Castleford side was allowed to break up and Malcolm had to endure a relatively lean spell at a time when his playing days came to an end, but it wasn't long before a crop of very talented youngsters started to emerge at Castleford, giving Mal a team of real promise. His side had to endure the despair of three Challenge Cup semi-final defeats in four years though, before their promise came to fruition in 1986, when Malcolm guided them to Wembley. The opponents, and favourites, were Hull KR, but Mal kept his 100 per cent record at the stadium intact as they won the trophy in a thrilling final.

Malcolm stayed with Cas for just one more season before Great Britain gave him the chance to coach the national side. He was unable to break the Aussie stranglehold on world rugby, but his teams tried hard and he did as well as any that have filled the role in recent years. Coaching stints at Leeds and Halifax followed, before Mal returned to Australia with the Newcastle Knights. It came as no surprise when Malcolm brought success to another club, and he led the Knights to a Grand Final victory. No one else had played for and coached sides to success in both the Challenge Cup and the Grand Final – a fitting testimony to a Rugby League legend.

Dean Sampson
Prop forward, 1987-present

Appearances: 327(92)

Tries: 68

Goals: 0

Drop Goals: 0

Points: 272

Previous club: Local junior rugby

(Statistics to end of May 2002)

One of the most popular players with the Castleford faithful in recent years, if not the club's history, Dean Sampson is still playing a starring role at the Jungle – in what he insists will be his last season as a player. The Sampson dynasty started at Castleford back in 1978, when David Sampson, a thirty-two-year-old prop forward, signed for the club from Bramley. Twenty-four years later, it continues with his son, Dean, both playing and coaching with the Tigers. Dean, a prop like his dad, was given his Castleford debut by Dave, after Sampson senior had taken over the Tigers' coaching role from Malcolm Reilly. However, there was no nepotism involved; Dean deserved his chance, and he has proved that well over 400 times since his signing from Stanley Rangers ARL.

Dean's Cas debut came in August 1987, and it was a try-scoring one against St Helens – the first of many top performances against the Merseyside club over the ensuing years. His first season got even better with a Yorkshire Cup final substitute appearance against Bradford in a draw at Headingley and another shot in the replay, which, unfortunately, only yielded a runners-up medal. However, he soon added to that with an international call-up by

the Great Britain Under-21 selectors – Dean made his representative debut against France and scored a try. It was to be his only appearance at that level though, setting a trend of underachieving on the representative front. This was purely down to the selectors, whose decisions over the years have mystified more than just Castleford fans. Dean did go on to make further appearances on the representative stage – but certainly not to the extent that he deserved.

Just a couple of years after making his senior debut, Dean had established himself as a regular in the Castleford line-up and, with Kevin Ward and the newly-arrived Lee Crooks at the club by the beginning of 1990, that was in the face of some strong competition. In fact, by the beginning of the following campaign, 1990/91, Castleford felt able to release Ward. After missing out on a Yorkshire Cup winner's medal in his first season, Dean collected one in 1990 and again in 1991, as the Tigers dominated the County competition. However, by the time the 1992 Challenge Cup trail came around, Dean was finding himself on the substitutes bench more often than not. Aussie signing Graeme Bradley had moved from the centre to the second row, and Keith England in turn moved forward to the front row, which meant that someone had to drop out. Unluckily for Dean, it was him, but he played a prominent part on the march to Wembley and, although again starting on the bench for the final, an injury to skipper Lee Crooks brought Dean into action as early as the thirty-third minute. Unfortunately, by the time of his arrival, the Tigers were already 0-12 down and, despite a second-half fight-back, the cup was retained by Wigan. There was some consolation for Dean though, when he won a late call to join the injury-hit Great Britain tourists in New Zealand, but he didn't make the Test team, appearing in just two matches – against Auckland and Canterbury.

With strong competition Dean alternated between a starting place and a spot on the bench over the next couple of seasons and, although he was never out of the senior squad, he picked up a winner's medal playing for the Alliance team that won the 1993 Yorkshire Senior Competition Cup. However, when Cas reached a major final once again, the 1994 Regal Trophy, he had to be content with a place on the bench, although he was called into the fray on that memorable afternoon at Headingley. Dean was in the starting line up when Castleford took the field at Old Trafford for the 1994 Premiership final though, and he scored the first try of the match in a towering performance, but it wasn't enough to stop Wigan, who gained revenge for their Regal Trophy final defeat.

When Dean impressed for Castleford against the 1994 Australian tourists, many good judges felt that he would meet them again in a Great Britain jersey. Writing in the *Evening Post*, Trevor Watson said: 'Sampson made his case for higher things'. But the call never came, despite the fact that eight different props played for Britain in the three Tests against the Aussies. Later in the season, after winning the Man of the Match award in the Regal Trophy quarter-final against Leeds (whose side included GB coach Ellery Hanley), Dean, not surprisingly, said: 'I wanted to show Hanley that I can play a bit'. Like the Castleford fans, he must have wondered just what he had to do.

Dean Sampson in thoughtful mood, reflecting on his 400 appeerances for the club in 2001.

Dean Sampson celebrates his hat-trick of tries against Huddersfield in 2001.

A call might have come his way for the England side that season, but, unfortunately, a four-match ban ruled him out.

Dean spent the summer of 1995 playing for Parramatta in Australia and, on his return, his international chance came when new coach Phil Larder named his squad for the Centenary World Cup competition. His senior representative debut came, at long last, against Fiji, and he won further caps against South Africa and, in the competition semi-final, against Wales. However, even then he was unlucky, as he missed out for the final against the Aussies.

The opening two Super League seasons (in 1996 and 1997) weren't the best for Castleford, but Dean was a model of consistency, and eventually won a Great Britain cap when he was a first Test substitute against the 1997 Australians at Wembley. Despite approaching the veteran stage, Dean was improving with age and, in 1999, he made the end-of-season 'Super League Dream Team'. Unfortunately, the season had its disappointments for Dean, as Cas lost out at the semi-final stage in both the Challenge Cup and the Grand Final, and he knew that those opportunities weren't going to come around too many more times. However, after making the 'Dream Team', he also won a recall to the England team for their two clashes with France, starting both and scoring tries in both. He also signed a two-year extension to his Castleford contract taking him to the end of the 2001 campaign, when, he said, he would retire.

No one was surprised when he didn't. Dean made his 400th appearance for the Tigers against Huddersfield in July 2001 and, a month later, he decided on another year at Cas. The change of heart delighted Castleford fans, who didn't want to lose their favourite, and he certainly hasn't let them down in 2002. He is earmarked to take on a full-time junior development role at Castleford when his playing days end, and there couldn't be a better role model, but he will leave a massive gap in the Tigers' ranks and it will take, in every sense, a very big man to fill it.

John Sheridan
Centre/loose forward, 1955-1966

Appearances: 300(1)

Tries: 86

Goals: 2

Drop Goals: 1

Points: 264

Previous club: Local junior rugby

John Sheridan was a tremendous servant to Castleford as both a player and a coach, but he never won a trophy and he was never selected for representative honours as a senior player. The centre had won junior honours for Yorkshire though, and he had been an England reserve when Castleford signed him from Lock Lane in the mid-1950s. His signing caused something of a stir, as Hunslet claimed that John had signed for them. However, in fact, he had only signed on second or, as it was known, 'A' team, forms, and his move to Castleford went through. He didn't have to make an 'A' team appearance for Cas though, as he was drafted straight into the first team to make a try-scoring debut against Workington in August 1955.

In season 1957/58, John was Castleford's leading try-scorer with 27 touchdowns, and it was in 1958 that he came closest to the representative honours that he deserved when he was a member of the Yorkshire 'Shadow' team. Had John played for a more 'fashionable' side than Castleford were at the time, representative honours would almost certainly have come his way.

John was made club captain in 1958/59 – the season that saw him switch from centre to the loose-forward position – but he filled either role with equal aplomb, and he

continued to be a key player as Castleford finally started to emerge from a period of very little success, the local youngsters starting to make their presence felt. However, as his own playing days began to draw to a close, he was given the role of 'A' team coach for the 1964/65 season, and he made a tremendous success of the job.

He continued in that role until 1981/82, although there was a two-year break, firstly when he was handed the first-team coaching job in 1973. Castleford ended the campaign in ninth place in the First Division, but John was to quit as head coach less than a year after taking on the job. The man who had been such a huge success in developing youngsters from the junior ranks, and who, in the previous year, had led the club's second team to a cup and League double, was taking undeserved flak from the terraces at Wheldon Road. The criticism became quite unpleasant, and John said: 'It's time to quit'.

After leaving Cas, John moved to Leeds to take their 'A' team coaching job, with no little success. But with Malcolm Reilly back at Castleford as the senior coach, John

John Sheridan in action at Headingley.

was soon to return home, where he again picked up the reins of the second string. During his time as 'A' team coach, John's teams won no less than nine Yorkshire Senior Competition Championships and six Yorkshire Senior Competition Cups, as well as guiding a host of young players through the early stages of their career. He had a skill that is hard to put a price on.

After leaving Cas, John did a wonderful job at perennial strugglers Doncaster, before working on the administrative side of the game with the Colts set-up. His knowledge of the game is immense, and you suspect that, to this day, it is something that is tapped into and passed on to those who ask.

John Sheridan is still passing on his Rugby League knowledge.

Peter Small
Centre three-quarter, 1958-1969

Appearances: 310(5)

Tries: 109

Goals: 0

Drop Goals: 0

Points: 327

Previous club: Local junior rugby

If nothing else, and it certainly won't be the case, Peter Small will be remembered for being Castleford's second ever tourist to Australasia, and, in 1962, the first for twenty-six years, following on from Arthur Atkinson, who toured in 1932 and again in 1936.

Peter joined Cas from local side Allerton Bywater in November 1958, and made his first-team debut a little over a month later, on Boxing Day, in the cauldron of Post Office Road. The story goes that Peter only went along to watch his new side tackle Featherstone, but was called into action. Unfortunately, it was a losing start, as Rovers won the local derby, but it didn't do Peter any harm, as he kept his place in the side to become a regular for many years to come.

His early days at Castleford were during a time when they were at the lower end of the table, although he was always a consistent player for his club, and one of the side's top performers. Nevertheless, Small was something of a surprise choice for Great Britain's 1962 tour to Australia and New Zealand, but he acquitted himself well on the tour. He didn't make the Test team in Australia, playing instead in ten games against the country and regional sides that the tourists faced, but, on the Kiwi leg of

the tour, he was selected for the second Test team against New Zealand, and scored a try for his country in their 8-27 defeat. That was to prove to be Small's one and only cap though, but as he also played in the three matches that the tourists played in South Africa, scoring three tries, Peter had represented both his club and country his well. A year later, Small was to get the chance to face the Aussies and play on the winning side, when Castleford entertained the 1963 tourists, and he was in their side that pulled off a tremendous and unexpected 13-12 victory.

As his career moved on, Small made what seemed to be the natural switch to the back row; a switch that proved a wise move by whoever instigated it. He was loose forward for Cas when they won their first trophy for many years in season 1966/67 in the new BBC 2 Floodlit competition, and he was in the second row a year later when they retained the cup. That move into the back row continued to pay dividends and, some five years after that test match appearance, Small won a second representative call when he was selected for the

Peter Small is about to score.

Yorkshire County side to face the 1967 Australian tourists. Again he was a winner against the Aussies, as the White Rose bloomed to record a 15-14 win at Belle Vue. Peter was in Castleford's 1968 Yorkshire Cup final team that lost to Leeds, but it was his last medal chance with the club.

Greater glory was beckoning for Castleford, but Small wasn't to be part of it, leaving the club on the eve of the 1969 cup campaign. His last match came against Huddersfield in January of that year, before a transfer to Hull KR. Peter ended his playing career at Bradford Northern.

Peter in action for Great Britain on the 1962 tour.

Bob Spurr
Hooker, 1968-1983

Appearances: 299(24)

Tries: 45

Goals: 0

Drop Goals: 0

Points: 135

Previous club: Local junior rugby

Bob Spurr followed in a long tradition at Castleford of honest and loyal club-men. Whilst the phrase 'never gave less than 100 per cent' is often overused, that certainly isn't the case with Bob. He started playing Rugby League as a youngster at Temple Street Junior School in Castleford and, although he then played Union for Castleford Grammar School in the morning, he would often play League with Glasshoughton Under-19s in the afternoon. Bob then switched to the Castleford Juniors side, and he was earmarked by the senior club as a future scrum-half, his regular position at the time. But first he first had a spell with Normanton Under-19s, representing Yorkshire at that level before signing professional forms with Cas in July 1968.

At this point, Bob was still playing at scrum-half and, six months on, it was in that position that he made his first-team debut. However, by the following season, after an inspired switch by coach John Sheridan, he had made the move to the hooking role – a position that he was to fill with distinction for Castleford over many years. Having said that, as he fought for a first-team place, Bob did move around occasionally, and he notched a hat-trick of tries for the senior side from the loose-forward position against Bramley in 1970. He was unable to make the breakthrough to the first team on a regular basis

though, but was winning medals as Castleford's 'A' team were enjoying no little success. However, the lack of senior opportunities was causing Bob some concern and, in season 1972/73, he asked to be put on the transfer list. Thank goodness there were no takers, even at the bargain price of £1,500! Bob continued to play consistently well for the second team, even though on the list, and his reward came midway the following season when he was elevated to the senior side as hooker, and this time he held on to that hard won spot. In fact, by the following year, 1974, Bob was given a call-up by Yorkshire – the first of two caps for the County side. Those were to be Bob's only senior representative honours, but they were hard won, and probably the more sweeter because of that.

Medals were starting to come Bob's way though, starting with an Embassy Sevens win in April 1976, then a BBC Floodlit Trophy success in December that year, followed by a Player's No. 6 final win a month later. Whilst he might not have been winning the Man of the Match awards in those cup wins, Bob was filling the role of unsung hero, so vital to any successful side. He was soon collecting

Bob Spurr in action against Halifax.

another winner's medal, after helping Cas defeat local rivals Featherstone in the 1977 Yorkshire Cup final.

Six years after making his Yorkshire debut, he won that second cap, playing against Cumbria in the 1980 County Championship and, despite the fact that there was growing pressure from rising star Kevin Beardmore, Bob was still holding his first-team place. A second Yorkshire Cup winner's medal was won in the 1981 final, and Bob's commitment to Cas brought him financial reward later that season when the club's fans showed their appreciation resulting in a well-deserved club record benefit cheque, handed to him by Rugby League fan and actor Colin Welland.

As it always does at some stage, time caught up with Bob, and the 1982/83 campaign saw Kevin Beardmore take over the first-team hooking spot. But for Bob, back in the 'A' team, there were more medals to be won, as Cas won the cup and Championship double. However, that was to be his last hurrah at Castleford and, in August 1983, fifteen years after joining Castleford, Bob made the short move to Featherstone. In all of that time, Bob hadn't just been an honest and loyal player, although he did enjoy those attributes. He was also a very good player, whose tackling and support play was first class – and it was, in his case, 100 per cent, week in week out.

Graham Steadman

Appearances: 209(28)

Tries: 121

Goals: 174

Drop Goals: 8

Points: 840

Previous club: Featherstone Rovers

The current Castleford coach, Graham Steadman, arrived somewhat belatedly at his hometown club, but he more than made up for lost time. 'Steady' started his professional career with York and playing for the Minstermen in 1984, he should have made Castleford sit up and take notice, if they hadn't before. The match was a cup tie that Cas were expected to win easily against Second Division opponents, but they reckoned without a battling display from York, and, in particular, their stand-off Steadman. He scored all his side's points, two tries and three goals, and Cas were unceremoniously dumped off the Wembley trail. However, when Graham became available, Castleford didn't move in, and Featherstone paid York £55,000 for his services. At Post Office Road, Steady became a big star, and, not surprisingly, they weren't too happy when, three years after they had bought him from York, their fierce local rivals did start showing an interest in their man.

Graham was keen to make the move though, and agreed terms with Cas, prompting Rovers to put an £185,000 fee on his head, and then suggest that Castleford had made an illegal approach. While the arguments raged, Graham himself was in Australia, having joined the Gold Coast Giants for the summer. In response to the fee

that Rovers were asking, Cas offered £100,000, but that was rejected and the issue went to a Rugby League tribunal. Two weeks later, they announced their decision. Castleford's previous record transfer fee had been the £11,500 they had paid Wakefield for George Ballantyne in 1978, but that was smashed as they agreed to pay the price that tribunal had set – £145,000, plus another £25,000 if, at any time in the future, Steadman won a Great Britain cap. Despite the fact that Graham had only one Yorkshire cap to his name when he joined Cas, a future international call-up was almost inevitable.

Graham quickly showed his worth, hitting the headlines almost from day one. A month after his move, he represented Yorkshire, scoring two tries and four goals as Lancashire were thrashed and, by the end of his first season, he had won his expected international call, kicking three goals for Great Britain in their shock defeat at the hands of France. Featherstone found themselves another £25,000 richer and, at £170,000, Graham became the world of Rugby League's costliest ever signing. His first year at Cas brought Graham 17 tries and 75 goals, and it was capped when he won a place in the Great Britain tour party for Papua and New Zealand. Graham won winner's medals in the 1990 and 1991 Yorkshire Cup finals, having moved to full-back between the two, and was awarded the Man of the Match award in the latter, after notching a final record points tally of sixteen. On the representative front, he was again selected by Yorkshire, and won two more British caps against France in 1992, before once again being named for the Lions squad bound for Australasia. But before that, Graham had the small matter of his first trip to Wembley, after Cas had fought their way to the cup final, with Graham scoring eight tries en route. The final was lost though, as Wigan proved too strong, but Graham had little time to dwell on the defeat as Australia beckoned. Before jetting out, he did have the chance to collect another accolade when he was presented with the First Division Player of the

Year award – voted for by his fellow professionals.

On tour, he was a tremendous success, capturing the full-back role for the Test matches in the face of stiff competition in the British squad, and shining especially in the win in Melbourne. However, back in the UK, an early injury to his foot saw Graham miss a large chunk of the 1992/93 campaign. He was back for the cup run, which ended at the quarter-final stage, but missed that year's internationals, when he would have been a certainty to win a few more caps. The following season was to bring major success for Steady and Castleford though. Graham was a try-scorer in all four rounds of the Regal Trophy, as the Tigers booked their place in the final at Headingley, with hot favourites Wigan lined up to meet them. However, Castleford completely upset the odds to thrash Wigan and bring another medal for

Graham Steadman coaching Castleford in 2002.

Graham Steadman in action during the 1992 Challenge Cup final against Wigan.

Steady, and his next honour came just weeks later, as he was selected to be a member of the Great Britain Sevens squad that took part in the Coca-Cola World competition. Another GB call-up came for the match against France, with the only blot on a tremendous season coming when Cas were defeated by Wigan in the Premiership final at Old Trafford.

Season 1994/95 saw the Aussies in the UK, but Jonathan Davies was holding down the British full-back place, and Graham only faced the Kangaroos in the second Test when Davies was out injured. It was his tenth GB cap, but it was to prove his last. However, it was another good campaign on the club front, as Cas finished third in the table, only to become embroiled in the Super League row at the season's end. The shortened 1995/96 campaign was Graham's last as a regular, and in Super League One, he made just seven starts – it was almost the end of a long and distinguished career.

Graham retired as a player at the end of the 1997 relegation battle campaign, when, at thirty-five, he was the oldest player in Super League. During his career, he amassed over 2,000 points in the game, with 239 tries and 542 goals. He said at the time: 'It was my childhood ambition to play for Castleford and I have had eight great years'.

But that was only chapter one in Graham's association with the Tigers. After calling it a day on the field, Graham worked alongside Aussie coach Stuart Raper and, when Stuart made the move to Wigan in May 2001, Graham was the obvious choice as his replacement. Graham has made rapid strides on the coaching front, not just at Cas but also as part of the Yorkshire and Great Britain set-ups. He had a great playing career for both club and country, and many good judges believe that he will go on to emulate that success on the coaching front.

Gary Stephens
Scrum-half, 1969-1980

Appearances: 262(10)

Tries: 78

Goals: 1

Drop Goals: 3

Points: 240

Previous club: Local junior rugby

Another of the highly talented half-backs that graduated to the Castleford first team via the ranks of the local schools and junior clubs, Gary Stephens always looked set to have a top career in Rugby League. His first representative call came at the tender age of fourteen, when he played for the Yorkshire Schools side, and was a foretaste of many more to come. Gary signed for Cas in 1969, and before graduating to the first team, he had won Championship and Cup medals with the club's 'A' team. By 1974, he was established in the senior squad and, at the end of that season, he was selected as the Castleford Supporters' Club Player of the Year. Although just twenty-one, it was a measure of Gary's progress that many were surprised when England didn't select him for the 1975 World Championship. Later that year, he was to emulate his achievement as a schoolboy when he made his senior Yorkshire County debut against Lancashire. Success overseas followed success at home, when Gary guested with Manly in Australia, capping an impressive stint by winning the Man of the Match award when the Sea Eagles triumphed in the Grand Final. Club honours with Cas came Gary's

way in the 1976/77 Floodlit and, as Man of the Match, in the Player's Trophy successes, and another couple of Yorkshire appearances were the reward for an outstanding season.

In 1977, Gary spent another summer guesting with Manly, returning in time to win yet another medal, when Castleford triumphed in the Yorkshire Cup final. A year on, and more honours were won, as Gary's form continued to impress the representative selectors, with another Yorkshire appearance in the 1978 County Championship and an international debut when Gary was capped by England against Wales in March 1979. But the pinnacle of Gary's representative career came at the end of that season when he was named in the 1979 Great Britain tour party for Australia and New Zealand. The wait had been long for Gary, who said: 'It was agony, I've spent twelve months preparing myself for this.' But he must have felt that it was worth it, after a highly successful trip saw Gary feature in five of the six Tests played by Britain. Back home, he was honoured to be named as captain of Yorkshire, when the County side tackled Lancashire on his home ground of Wheldon Road. Another season ended with well-deserved recognition for Gary, as both the sponsors and the supporters of Castleford awarded him their 1979/80 Player of the Year awards.

Not a year had passed without Gary receiving some sort of honour or accolade and, in 1980, he celebrated a well-earned benefit, jointly with his often half-back partner Phil Johnson, as well as winning his sixth County cap. But there were some talented young number sevens coming through the ranks at Castleford and, towards the end of the year, there was speculation that Wigan, who were in the Second Division and desperate for promotion at the time, were interested in taking him to Central Park. The rumours proved to be much more than that, and a bid of £35,000, a record fee for Castleford, secured his services. Gary spent four years at Wigan and a season at Leigh, before crossing back over the Pennines to Halifax. That proved a tremendous move, as it brought Gary a first Wembley appearance and a winner's medal in 1987, at the age of thirty-four. It wasn't quite the end of Gary's playing career, as he had a very brief flirtation with Leeds, before taking on the player-coach job at York.

It was in the coaching role that Gary returned to Castleford in 1996, as assistant to John Joyner, but it was a short stay, with Gary leaving along with John the following year. Gary's son, Gareth, also had a spell as a player with Castleford and, although he was a more than useful player, who also played for Leeds, he was unable to match his father's achievements. Gary was a very hard act to follow.

Gary Stephens in action during the 1977 Yorkshire Cup final.

Nathan Sykes

Prop forward, 1991-present

Appearances: 153(76)

Tries: 8

Goals: 0

Drop Goals: 0

Points: 32

Previous club: Huddersfield junior rugby

(Statistics to end of May 2002)

In the changing world of Rugby League, with much greater freedom of movement for players, a benefit for ten or more years' service has become a rarity. However, the Tigers' prop, Nathan Sykes, is someone who fully deserved to earn one, continuing a Castleford tradition of long and loyal service to the club. Nathan joined the Tigers from Huddersfield-based Moldgreen ARL Under-16s side in May 1991, as a much sought-after young player. Wigan and Leeds were reported to be just two of the clubs that he knocked back to sign for the Tigers, who, under coach Darryl Van De Velde, were quite a fashionable club at the time. His own coach at Moldgreen said at the time of his signing that Nathan could 'go all the way', and he has proved his former mentor to be a very good judge.

Nathan had picked up one award long before turning professional though, as a member of the Huddersfield Schools team that played in the curtain-raiser for the 1985 Challenge Cup final at Wembley. He wasn't much more than a schoolboy when Cas handed him a first-team debut a week after his seventeenth birthday, taking the chance of a Yorkshire Cup tie with Batley to give the

youngster a baptism. It was to be his only senior appearance that year as he learnt his trade, but he proved later that he was learning it well. The following season saw Nathan make just five substitute appearances for the first team, and season 1993/94 was much the same, but he did make the first of six Great Britain Academy appearances against France in 1993 and, later that year, he played for the Yorkshire Academy side against the Junior Kiwis. Just a couple of weeks later, Nathan was back at Wembley, this time making his second appearance for the GB Academy side, who also played the Junior Kiwis as a curtain-raiser to the Great Britain v. New Zealand Test. Before the year was out, Nathan had been elevated to the Great Britain Under 21s side which faced France – and he was still just nineteen years of age. Representative honours were coming thick and fast and, by the end of the season, along with team-mate Chris Smith, Nathan was selected for the Great Britain Academy squad to tour Australia. Whilst Nathan didn't get too many senior chances that season, he came on as a substitute in the 1993/94 Premiership final at Old Trafford, and although his side lost, he scored a try at the 'Theatre of Dreams'.

By the following season, Nathan was becoming a regular in the Tigers' squad, and he won his second Under-21 cap playing for

Nathan Sykes in action in the 2002 Challenge Cup semi-final against Wigan.

the British youngsters against the Australian tourists. Nathan was also maturing into a fine prop, who set a high level of consistency in his performance. He was a cornerstone of the Tigers back in 1999 when they reached two semi-finals, and his reward came at the end of that term with a call from England coach John Kear and a full international debut against France to complete his set of caps at all levels. In 2000, he signed a new three-year deal with Castleford, and managed to grab two tries and avoid having to repeat his 'nude run' of 1999 – a 'task' for any Castleford first-team player who doesn't score a try throughout the season. Super League Six in 2001 saw Nathan win his second England cap against Wales at Wrexham, and he was unlucky, as a member

of the Great Britain squad preparing to face the Aussie tourists, to miss the cut when the numbers were trimmed. However, there was some consolation in winning the club's Player of the Year and the Players' Player of the Year awards at the season's end. In 2002, Nathan was given another representative boost with a Yorkshire County debut in the Origin fixture. Reaching a benefit often signifies the end of a career, but when Nathan was awarded his, he was still only twenty-seven, with plenty of time to win more honours. As a top player and a good club-man, no one would argue that he didn't deserve them.

Thomas Taylor

Prop forward, 1931-1946

Appearances: 389

Tries: 17

Goals: 0

Drop Goals: 0

Points: 51

Previous club: Local junior rugby

Tommy Taylor was described by Len Garbett, Castleford's much respected club president, as one of the 'quietest, most modest, respected gentleman players to have been a success in Rugby League'. Coming from Len, who has seen and known most of those who have ever donned the black and amber of Cas, that is praise indeed. Indeed, Tommy was respected by both his Castleford team-mates and by all of those who played against him.

Tommy made his first-team debut, in the open-side prop position, against Batley in March 1932. It was a winning start, and he went on to spend fifteen years with Castleford, making almost 400 appearances for the club. In all of those matches, Tommy was never once sent from the field – a distinction that very few props could claim, including many who have made far fewer appearances.

Tommy was amongst Castleford's most consistent players in his many years at the club, but after picking up a Yorkshire County cap early in his career, he had to wait a long time for further representative honours. That first Yorkshire appearance came in 1935 against Lancashire, but he had to wait ten years before picking up a further two caps. It was also in 1945, some thirteen years after making his senior club debut, that Tommy represented his country for the first time, playing for England against Wales in Swansea. As they say, everything comes to he who waits! Unfortunately for Tommy, after all those years, he was on the losing side.

During the Second World War, when Castleford, amongst others, didn't field a team for a couple of seasons, some other clubs continued playing. One was Huddersfield, and Tommy guested with the Fartown club for two terms. When he left Castleford, after playing his last match for them against Wakefield in 1946, Huddersfield were quick to take him back.

Finally, no mention of Tommy would be complete without reference to hooker Harold Haley and fellow prop Pat McManus – his front-row partners in the 1935 Challenge Cup win. The trio were magnificent servants, who made a combined total of no less than 1,023 appearances for Castleford.

Tommy Taylor, one of the thirteen players who brought the Challenge Cup to Castleford for the first time in 1935.

Darryl Van De Velde

Head coach, 1988-1993

Appearances: 0

Tries: 0

Goals: 0

Drop Goals: 0

Points: 0

Previous club: Redcliffe (Australia)

Darryl Van De Velde was the Castleford coach from July 1988 to March 1993.

Australian Darryl Van De Velde became Castleford's first overseas coach when he was brought to the club in 1988. In his first season in charge, Cas looked set for their first ever title, as they won eleven and drew one of their opening twelve matches. They also defeated Huddersfield 94-12 in the Yorkshire Cup, setting a club record highest score but, sadly, the Tigers fell away as the second half of the season unfolded. However, it was the start of an exciting roller-coaster ride for the club under the big Queenslander and, despite bringing no major honours to the club, he lifted Castleford's profile like no one had done before him.

Darryl had made his mark with Redcliffe Dolphins club, taking them to the Brisbane Grand Final prior to linking up with Cas, but he found the door closed on his ambitions to try his hand with a Sydney club in the Big League. His aspirations were now on behalf of Castleford though, and he said on his arrival in England: 'The chairman (David Poulter) wants success and he was the main reason I decided to come here'. Indeed, he made his mark

before he had even landed. Australian Test star Gary Belcher was being courted by both Cas and Halifax, but he opted for the Tigers when Van De Velde was appointed. Belcher didn't play too many games for Castleford, but he was a quality signing. Darryl made no changes in personnel throughout his first season, though, preferring to give the squad he had inherited their chance. However, he did later suggest that he perhaps should have done, as the blistering start to the season came to an end – but things were to change during his second term of office.

In one stroke, Castleford's record transfer fee was lifted from £11,500 to a world record £170,000, when Graham Steadman was signed and, later in the season, Lee Crooks was brought in for a £150,000 fee. Both players proved to be worth every penny, serving Castleford tremendously well long after Darryl's departure, but they weren't the only new faces. Ian Bragger was signed from Salford for £60,000, St John Ellis was brought in as part of a £30,000 deal, whilst a £90,000 bid for loose forward Gary Divorty was rejected by Hull. It was the first, and last, time that Castleford have ever been given the title of big spenders, but fans loved seeing their club making news. On the field, although

Castleford weren't making the headlines that their spending was, in winning their last ten matches, there were clear signs that a top-class team was emerging. The following year, those investments, apart from Bragger, who was unable to make his mark, started to bear fruit. Under Van De Velde, Cas were not only winning, they were playing some good rugby, as illustrated by their 42-12 demolition of holders Bradford at the quarter-final stage of the 1990 Yorkshire Cup. 'Bradford had no answer to Castleford's superb attacking rugby', reported the *Yorkshire Post*. Hull KR were 'swept aside' in the semi-final, and although it was a tougher than expected match, Wakefield were defeated in the final to give Darryl his first trophy.

Castleford finished the season a creditable fourth in the table and, in the build-up to the 1991/92 season, Darryl continued his re-shaping. Castleford's line-up became even more star-studded with the capture of Kiwi internationals Tawera Nikau and Richie Blackmore and Great Britain tourist Mike Ford. The Tigers breezed through to another Yorkshire Cup final success, and then came the coach's greatest success, as he guided his side to Wembley. Opponents Wigan had won the Challenge Cup in the previous four campaigns and were the dominant force in the game – a brave performance wasn't enough from Cas, but they could reflect on a highly successful campaign, finishing third in the league behind only Wigan and Saints.

The 1992/93 season wasn't to prove as fruitful though, and Darryl's fifth season at Castleford was to be his last. His side was shaping up well in the Regal Trophy, dominating but losing the semi-final against Bradford, and similarly in the Challenge Cup, a tough away draw at Headingley in the quarter-final was there for the taking, but was allowed to slip away. However, a factor might have been that, on the eve of the game the Castleford, the players had learned that Darryl was heading home at the end of the season. His chance in the Aussie Big League had come, with new club Queensland Crushers appointing him as

A smiling Darryl Van De Velde at Wheldon Road. Darryl brought a smile to the faces of Cas fans with some top signings.

their chief executive. It was an opportunity he couldn't pass up.

It seems Darryl was to miss the hands-on coaching role though, and ultimately he moved back into that arena. That was in England, briefly with Huddersfield and then with Warrington for four years, up to 2001. Although he probably didn't achieve the success he would have wished for, Darryl always added something to the clubs he was connected with, and his greatest testimony is surely the number of top players who have been happy to say that he is the best coach that they have ever worked with.

Adrian Vowles

Loose forward, 1997-2001

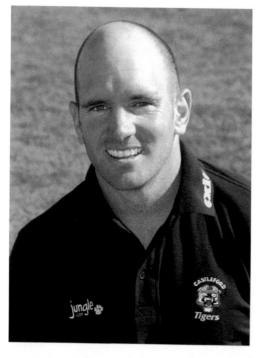

Appearances: 142

Tries: 33

Goals: 1

Drop Goals: 1

Points: 135

Previous club: North Queensland Cowboys (Australia)

Adrian Vowles arrived at Castleford with a good reputation, but he left it with a much better one, and that was despite the fact that he moved to archrivals Leeds! Vowles had made over seventy first-grade appearances in his native Australia, playing for the now defunct Gold Coast Seagulls and the North Queensland Cowboys. In his last year with the Cowboys, Adrian was appointed captain – gaining his first chance to develop the leadership qualities that stood out so well in his time at the Tigers. 'Vowlsey' was also Castleford's first Aussie signing for some time who had a State of Origin appearance to his name. He had won that coveted place with Queensland in 1994 and, adding to honour, the clash with New South Wales in Melbourne attracted a then record crowd in Australia of no less than 87,000. One of those people recommending Vowles was former coach Darryl Van De Velde – and, apparently, Darryl had also recommended Cas to Adrian.

So, he came with quite a pedigree, but in truth the Castleford fans didn't immediately warm to the Queenslander, as their side struggled during the early months of first campaign, but how things were to change.

Adrian came to play at stand-off in 1997, but the season got off to a bad start and initially became much worse. The Tigers just couldn't win in 1997, and very soon it became clear that relegation was a very real threat. However, the club reacted and brought in a new coach in Aussie Stuart Raper, and, slowly but surely, he turned things around. Adrian Vowles was one of those to pay tribute to the new boss when relegation was avoided and the club embarked upon a wholly unexpected Premiership run. In fact, their second round victory over the Bradford Bulls meant that Adrian's young twins were born in England rather than Australia. Had the Tigers been defeated at Odsal and the season ended, he and his pregnant wife were set to return home and have the twins back in Oz. But Cas won, and Adrian had himself a couple of Pommies! The Premiership run ended at the semi-final stage, but Cas were on the way back and Adrian Vowles had played a major part, resulting, not surprisingly, in a new contract. It wasn't too long into the following campaign that he was signing an extension to that contract, as his drive, leadership and consistency were bringing interest from other clubs. 'I really wanted to stay at the Tigers, it's a great club', said Vowles. It was a surprise to no one when, at the season's end, both the club's Player of the Year award and that of the

Player's Player of the Year went the way of Adrian Vowles.

With Mike Ford leaving Cas at the close of the 1998 season, Adrian was the obvious choice as captain, and now settled in at loose forward, he led his side to their best campaign for many years in 1999. The Tigers marched into the Challenge Cup semi-final, only to be cruelly denied in the last minute by London. But they didn't allow that defeat to crush the spirit at the club, a spirit that Adrian epitomised, and, at the end of the season, two years after their brush with relegation, the Tigers were in the top five and the play-offs. Adrian led his charges superbly to away wins at Wigan and Leeds in those play-offs, before St Helens thwarted their Grand Final hopes at the semi-final stage. But for Adrian himself, there was still more glory, as he capped a tremendous campaign by winning the game's top individual honour – the Man of Steel award. No one argued with his selection. Typically, when receiving the award, he paid tribute to his team-mates, saying: 'We don't have a great deal of money down at Wheldon Road, but we are fighters'.

Although Castleford again made the play-offs in 2000, the season was something of an anti-climax after their two semi-finals in 1999, but Adrian was always there, leading by example and defying numerous knocks and bumps to lead from the front. At the end of the year, he was to receive a surprise World Cup call – but not from his native Australia. Unbeknown to him, his grandmother had originated from Scotland, and that qualified Adrian for the Scottish World Cup squad. He made his international debut for his adopted country in the World Cup, weighing in with three appearances. He again represented Scotland in 2001, but a disappointing season for the Tigers was to be Adrian's last at the club. Tigers fans had felt certain that he would end his playing career in England at the Jungle, even when rumours of his possible departure started to do the rounds.

However, they proved to be true – and the blow of his departure was made worse by the fact that he was to join Leeds – but Adrian had served the club tremendously for five years, never giving less than his best, and that view hasn't been diminished by his departure.

Left: Strapped up as usual, it never stopped Adrian from giving his best. *Right:* Adrian Vowles in action in 2001.

Johnny Ward

Hooker/prop forward, 1960-1970

Appearances: 259(3)

Tries: 42

Goals: 0

Drop Goals: 3

Points: 132

Previous club: Featherstone Rovers

Johnny Ward joined Castleford on a free transfer, yet when he left the club ten years later, it caused the chairman to resign. Castleford signed Wardy in 1960, and although no fee was involved, it turned into one of the most astute captures that the club have ever made. It is doubtful that it was intended as such, but close rivals Featherstone did Cas a massive favour when they allowed Johnny Ward to leave. He was then a hooker and soon blossomed at Wheldon Road to the extent that, three years later, the 'free transfer man' was selected for Great Britain to play in the third Test against the 1963 Australia tourists at Headingley. The British side had lost the opening two Tests, the second very heavily, and, with the series lost, there were calls for new faces to be given a chance. One of those new faces was Johnny's, and he sealed his place with a masterly, and very timely, performance for Castleford against the Aussies, when he scored two tries as Cas sensationally beat the tourists 13-12. He added another try against the boys from Down Under in a most impressive Test debut, which went

the way of Great Britain, 16-5. In the New Year, Wardy was back in action for his country, playing twice in winning Test matches against France, but those were to be his last Test matches as a Castleford player. Wardy had proved himself as a top-class hooker, but a bad leg injury kept him out for a spell and, when he returned, he moved to the blind-side prop position – a switch that proved a revelation. Either side of the injury, he made four appearances for the Yorkshire County side, two as a hooker and two as a prop. His greatest skill in his new position was that of a being superb ball-handler. Johnny's trickery with the ball often left opponents and fans alike bemused, as few knew what he was going to do next, but he almost always managed to release the ball. Thankfully, his team-mates seemed to be in on the act!

In 1969, Johnny was part of Castleford's team that won at Wembley against Salford and played a big part in the Reds' downfall. Later that year, he was back in the international side, playing for England in matches against Wales and France.

But on the eve of the Castleford's defence of the Challenge Cup, fans were dealt a real blow. Despite achieving a great deal of success at Cas, Wardy had been looking for a change of club and was placed

Johnny Ward dives over for a try againts Australia at Wheldon Road.

on the transfer list, but with the cup approaching and no enquiries having been made, he was taken off the list early in 1970. 'I wanted a move, but couldn't see the point of remaining on the list at £6,000 when no club seemed interested in me', Ward told the *Daily Mirror*. But one club did decide that they wanted him, and that was Salford – the side he had helped to beat at Wembley nine months earlier. Johnny left for the Reds three days before the cup deadline, but he left behind him a boardroom row. Chairman Harry Clarkson quit the board in protest, claiming to 'Consider it wrong to part with a player of Ward's ability on the eve of the cup.' But it mattered not, and Castleford had lost both

a top player and their chairman. Thankfully, it didn't affect their cup chances, as Cas went on to win the trophy. Perhaps inevitably, they met Salford along the way. The tie was at the quarter-final stage, and Cas recorded a comfortable 15-0 win over the Reds, Wardy and all.

Johnny did achieve some success in three years at the Willows. He was a 1970 tourist, alongside five of his former colleagues, and won Player and Lancashire Cup medals, before a brief spell with Leeds at the end of his long and illustrious career.

Kevin Ward

Seond row/prop forward, 1978-1990

Appearances: 301(12)

Tries: 74

Goals: 0

Drop Goals: 0

Points: 249

Previous club: Local junior rugby

A hero to two sets of supporters in England and one in Australia – that's Kevin Ward. A magnificent prop forward, 'Wardy' was a late starter in the game, joining Cas from Stanley Rangers as a twenty-one-year-old in 1978. At the time, Kevin was a second-row forward, and he quickly made up for any lost time by establishing himself in the first team within a year of his signing. His strong running from the back row quickly made him a firm favourite, not least because he became a regular try-scorer, reaching double figures in his first four seasons – a very healthy return for a big forward.

Kevin's form was such that in little over a year on from turning professional, he was representing Great Britain Under-24's against France. He made two more GB appearances at that level, including when his country's young stars suffered a narrow defeat at the hands of the 1980 New Zealand tourists at Fulham's Craven Cottage. Two years later, Kevin had won Yorkshire County honours and, in 1984, he made his full Test-match debut in what was to prove an outstanding international

career. Kevin won seventeen Great Britain caps, with no less than nine of those Tests being against the all-conquering Australians. It was in the first series of those matches that he won the respect of the Aussies, which was later to see him playing Down Under and becoming one of the most popular 'Pommies' to do so.

Before that though, Wardy continued to be a rock in the Cas pack, making the switch to prop, and he was one of their big stars in the successful 1986 Wembley campaign.

A year later, he was to follow in the footsteps of his club coach, Mal Reilly, when he took the road from Castleford to the Manly Sea Eagles to play in the Aussie Big League. However, unlike his coach, who made a long-term switch, it was only as a 'guest' player in the English off-season. Kevin made just twelve appearances for Manly – but he made a massive impression in those dozen games. In truth, he joined a very good side, but he added to it, and reached the Grand Final with them. Although he was not the official Man of the Match in that game, many good judges in Australia felt that Kevin had deserved the award after a magnificent display in his side's defeat of the Canberra Raiders. Yet he only played in the match after making a return flight to Australia. Kevin had flown home to Cas after ending his short guest stint with Manly to start the new English campaign, but when the Sea Eagles reached their final, he was allowed to return. At that point, Kevin was regarded on either side of the globe as the world's best prop forward. And there were some very good ones in the game at the time.

In 1988, he returned to Australia as a Great Britain tourist, playing another handful of matches for Manly at the tour's conclusion. But by now, Darryl Van De Velde had taken over the coaching reins at Cas and, after sticking with those players he had inherited for his first season in charge, he started to make changes in his second. Lee Crooks was a big-money signing and, although still very much a regular, Kevin's form had dipped a little. With Lee on board, there was competition, and Kevin was made available for transfer

Kevin Ward in action in the 1986 Challenge Cup final.

'Wardy' drives forward against Bradford Northern.

in the 1990 off-season – a move felt by many Cas fans to have come somewhat prematurely. St Helens must have felt the same, as they soon stepped in to sign him, paying a reported fee of £80,000. Possibly Kevin needed a fresh challenge, and his new club gave him that opportunity and he rewarded them. He gave Saints three great seasons and won a clutch of new honours, including a Great Britain recall, along the way. The St Helens fans, as had those at Cas and Manly, took him to their hearts and were devastated when a nasty leg injury ended his career. The injury and later complications were to give Kevin problems for a few years after his retirement, but he has recovered and is now a welcome guest at Rugby League functions, where he is still revered by those who followed his career.

Appearances: 203(13)

Tries: 42

Goals: 0

Drop Goals: 0

Points: 126

Previous club: North's (Australia)

Geoff Wraith was a Belle Isle product, who played for Wakefield and then emigrated to Australia, before returning to England to join Castleford. The classy full-back had been a star with Wakefield Trinity over a number of years before, in 1973, he and his wife emigrated to Australia, where Geoff continued his rugby career with the Norths club in Brisbane. His move Down Under was seen as a surprise, as he had been on the verge of selection for Great Britain, but the Sunshine State had its own attraction. However, Cas chairman Phil Brunt, who was in Australia with Great Britain for the 1975 World Championships, persuaded Geoff to return to England and life at Wheldon Road. Geoff was certainly in demand, as Hull KR were also hot on his heels, but he opted for Cas and was a great success.

Geoff slotted in well to a Cas side that was on the way up and, after only eight matches for his new club, he was called up by Yorkshire. He made a second County appearance a month later and, at the end of the season, Geoff was a member of the Castleford Sevens side, who took the Embassy Trophy at Headingley. Geoff was a strong last line of defence, but he also had plenty of pace in attack, which he used to good effect, with nine tries in that first campaign back home. The following year, Geoff got his hands on two more winner's medals, as Castleford tasted double trophy success in the Floodlit Competition and the Player's No. 6 tournament. He was again given the call by Yorkshire and was one of five Cas men in the County side that played Cumbria. He continued to find his way from full-back to the try-line with ten touchdowns. The honours kept on coming, as 1977/78 yielded Geoff his fourth winner's medal in three years at Castleford, as the Tigers clinched the Yorkshire Cup against Featherstone.

By 1979 Geoff, now in his thirty-second year, was playing as well as ever, and when he picked up the *Sunday People* Player of the Month award, there was serious talk of a place in the Great Britain touring party for the forthcoming trip to Australia. But that wasn't to be, although there was some consolation when he was selected as the Castleford Player of the Season – a thoroughly well-deserved award. Despite now approaching the veteran stage, Geoff was still in the minds of some selectors as he made the 'shadow' squad for Yorkshire's

Bob Bearmore gets a pass away to Geoff Wraith against Hull in 1981.

1979 County Championship clash with Lancashire. But after another consistent season, he came out of the shadows at the start of the 1980/81 campaign to regain his place in Yorkshire's starting line-up against both Cumbria and Lancashire. At thirty-four years of age, Geoff was to score what many described as the best try in his long career, when Cas just lost out 11-12 to Hull in a magnificent 1981 Premiership semi-final tie. Bob Beardmore made a splendid break from a scrum, sprinting over sixty yards before being hauled down, but he found none other than Geoff Wraith at his shoulder, and the full-back held off the cover to touch down. Writing in the *Evening Post*, Trevor Watson said: 'When you consider that Wraith had been behind his own line when the scrum formed, it was a fabulous run by a player whose grey hairs outnumber the dark ones these days.' Once again, Geoff was picking up an award at the season's end, this time as the sponsor's Player of the Season.

However, as the following year's campaign got underway, Geoff wasn't able to command a regular place in the Castleford starting line-up, but that didn't stop him from passing on his experience to the second team, and he was once again amongst the medals as Cas 'A' team won the Yorkshire Senior Competition Cup. At the end of that campaign, his seventh at Castleford, Geoff announced his retirement as a player. A very popular and loyal player, Geoff was appointed as assistant coach to Malcolm Reilly after his retirement, earning wide respect in that role. So much so, that after two years in the post, he was offered, and accepted, a senior coaching role – back at Wakefield, where it all began.